Dr. Priscilla Schelp and Richard Lee-Thai

Become your Superself!
Connect with Yourself to Connect with Others

DEDICATION

Richard and I want to thank our loving families and friends. We also want to thank everyone that helped us on the way to being a superconnector and the many fascinating people we met along the way!

We went to express our special thanks to our test readers that helped us making the most out of this book:

Dr. Anna-Elisa Goeke
Annish Saini
Chris Fenning
Denisa Millo
Evelyn Shaw Corley
Goldie Hartford
Isabel Blumenberg
Jana Vialon
Joan Barredo
Julia Kounlavong
Dr. Julian Hochrath
Kevin Pritchard
Kilian Jonasch
Linda Huang
Manel Haddadi
Marc Maegdefrau
Marc-René Simon
Pascal Lauria
Simon V. L. Pausewang
Dr. Staffan Hedén
Wolfhard Janz
Yvonne M. Diffenhard

Our editors:
Erin Bledsoe
Mandy Hindenburg

Thank you to some of the amazing clubs and partners of Priscilla`s start-up "networkx" that contributed to this book:

POLO BEAUTY GROUP

Content

Chapter 4 – Self-Care   44

Chapter 5 – Self-Development   68

About the Book Series

"I define connection as the energy that exists between people when they feel seen, heard, and valued; when they can give and receive without judgment; and when they derive sustenance and strength from the relationship."
— Dr. Brené Brown

When was the last time you truly felt connected? A time when you felt genuinely seen, heard, and valued as an individual? A time when you felt like you weren't being talked over, and that space was held for you to be your authentic self? It can seem elusive in this age of loneliness.

You may have heard of physical health and mental health, but have you heard of "social health"?
As defined by Kasley Killam, Founder of the Social Health Labs: "Social health is the dimension of well-being that comes from connection and community. Whereas physical health is about our bodies and mental health is about our minds, social health is about our relationships."

There is a whole missing dimension of wellbeing that was never talked about while growing up. School doesn't teach us how to make friends, be a good listener, or overcome shyness. The lack of education means people are often left to fend for themselves. Our social relationships are absolutely essential for our personal and professional lives. Many great minds echo this.

Esther Perel said, "The quality of your relationships determines the quality of your life." Jim Rohn pointed out, „You are the average of the five people you spend the most time with." This list could go on and on. This fundamental human need means that there ought to be better education about social health, so people can live fulfilling and meaningful lives.

There are many, many books, courses, and coaches available on the topic of connection and networking. So why should you care about this book series?

1. You get to solve the real problem! As with most challenges we face in life, we sometimes fail to connect with people deeply. A large reason for this is because of our own mental barriers. You might tell yourself that networking is not in your genes or that you will never be able to build connections with others. Most networking books are based on covering up these thoughts, treating them like they don't exist. And surprise, surprise, that is not fully effective. As a familiar speaking coach said, "Thoughts set muscles free," meaning you can pretend to be as self-confident or as open as you want, but other people will spot inconsistencies in your behavior and identify you as a fraud. People will not be able to pinpoint exactly what it is. However, much of the classical networking book advice, such as "Keep eye contact" and "Keep your hands out of your pockets," just won't do it. This first book lays the foundation by teaching you how to connect with yourself. This is the foundation you need to connect deeply to others.

2. You receive step-by-step guidance! The reasons and occasions in life for why you need to start building a new network are wide-ranging: You go to a new school, a new university, a new job, a new city or country, or your divorce, your partner passes away, and much more. This book series is unique because you learn how to network from scratch, from "0". In the second book, we provide you with a step-by-step guide on how to build your network through the different phases.

3. You learn to connect in the physical and the digital world! The rapid advancement of technology means that digital communication now forms the basis for many of our interactions with others. The COVID-19 pandemic led to people working and going to school from home. Zoom calls, online events, and interaction on platforms such as Clubhouse, online discussion forums, and social media increased. COVID-19 has accelerated the online movement. Some critics see Web3 and the Metaverse as the death of being sociable; however, we do not believe in resisting change. On the contrary, you need to embrace change and be ahead of the curve. If you are prepared and do it right, you can even make it your competitive advantage. Therefore, in the second book, we aim to teach you how to build a world-class network for both the physical and digital world. See the online world as a chance to connect with people you might never meet in person, where you can still collaborate and develop meaningful relationships. Doesn't that sound amazing?

4. We teach you how to become a super connector! Most books end with how you connect with others. But let us tell you, there is a level beyond just connecting with people. We do not stop at teaching you how you can connect with other people. In the third book we teach you how to add value to the world and other peoples' lives by connecting other people to each other!

EXPECTATION MANAGEMENT & READING ADVICE
Even though this book series is about how to build up a world-class network, this first book is not about you connecting to other people. This is not a networking book but rather a self-development book. It is about you and your relationship with yourself.
Remember the last time you had a bad day and went to an event to meet new people? It likely did not go that well,

because you were not feeling well. That is just one example of how you feel inside you affects how well you connect to other people.

With this book, we want that you are feeling well, you are fine with yourself, reflecting on your current and future interactions and connections with other people." With this book, we want that you are feeling well, you are fine with yourself, reflecting on your current and future interactions and connections with other people.

Technically seen, this is not a book and more like a handbook. But it is not enough to read it, you need to work with it. If you regularly do the exercises as suggested, this book will change your life. This handbook summarizes the most important teachings Richard and I have had throughout our life so far. It is the summary of what we read, heard, learned, and applied in our lives. We are no professional writers, just two people wishing to share their knowledge with others. Also, this book is not a scientific book. We decided against it, because we want to save you time reading through all kinds of theories. Instead, we want to provide you with the meat and exercises you can implement without becoming the next Sigmund Freud.

Richard and I wrote the book for our younger selves! So, if you are completely in touch with yourself and are super into self-acceptance, self-care, and development, you can skip this book and hand it over to someone that needs it more than you.
Richard and I had to learn and are still learning some of the lessons ourselves. We understand that we are always learning and growing. Richard contributed with theories and exercises but decided against sharing much personally.

However, I will get personal with you so you can relate and hopefully learn from me. Lastly, when I talk about my achievements, I am not aiming to brag. I want to show you that everything and anything is possible. I grew up normally, had ADD, and was destined for mediocracy. I decided not to accept that and aimed for a different life. I want to inspire you to do the same. Go for what you want, achieve what you want.

To make the most out of this book, we do not recommend only reading this book but again, working through it. Read one chapter, do the exercise, apply and train...then do the next chapter. Reading this book will not be life-changing, but applying the practices will!
For those of you who wish to do the exercises in a book, a workbook will also be available soon.

Chapter 1 – Introduction

You might be asking yourself why we wrote a whole book about your relationship with yourself. Firstly, it is to help everyone—just like it helped Richard and I change, grow and develop into the people we are now. I assume you are not entirely satisfied with the relationships in your life, which is why you bought this book. Or maybe you are an exception and have amazing relationships with other people that you want to make even better! If you are not currently satisfied with your relationships, it might be because you're not where you want to be with them. There is a gap between your reality and expectations.

You are most likely aware of what you are missing in your current social circle. Maybe you do not feel loved enough? Maybe you do not feel supported enough?

I call it the fairytale effect. You can see it in a lot of romantic and other relationships. I asked some of my single friends about the man of their dreams, and many tell me something like this: "Priscilla, I want a guy that is very good-looking, wealthy, takes care of me, has a white (not horse but) Porsche, and treats me like a princess." I stay quiet for a few seconds, then give them a looooong look and ask: "ARE you a princess?" They reply, "What do you mean?" Then I ask again, "Are YOU a princess?"

What do I want to highlight with this example? How can you expect a prince when you are not a princess? How can you expect a super fantastic person to want to be your friend if you don't match that commitment as a potential friend? The answer: You cannot! You usually attract people who share similar mindsets. That's why the more you strive to achieve your superself, the more likely you will attract other super people in your life!

1.1 Benefits of Connecting with Yourself

You might have a lot of BUTs in your mind—BUTs on why this book might not work for you. Your inner monologue might be saying: "I am just not that self-confident. I am not attractive, I am not successful enough to be happy with myself."

The scary thing is that whatever you believe can become a self-fulfilling prophecy. We are not our thoughts, but we can give them the power to shape our lives. Of course, there is nothing wrong with you having these types of thoughts. When we are born, we are blank slates and accumulate beliefs and behaviors through our environment. However, anything you have learned can also be unlearned. It does take intentional effort to reprogram your inner narrative, but the ultimate benefit at the end of it is that you can be fully accepting of yourself and not let external factors determine your self-worth.

Consider this: How likely will your life be substantially different a few months from now, if you don't change your relationship with yourself? What could be possible if you developed a better connection with yourself?
You can choose to do nothing and indulge in complaining or blaming yourself—it is the least risky road to take. Changing nothing requires no risk. BUT you also cannot win or gain anything by taking the risk!
Whatever thoughts arise, just notice them. Understand them. Then, try to pause them for a short while and give yourself a chance to begin an exciting and enjoyable journey that can completely change your life.

Connecting with yourself enables you to:
Get to know yourself better
Improve your self-confidence
Better protect your boundaries
Become better in self-care
Get more content and balance
Be happier with yourself and your life
Judge others less
Be more grateful
See the good in others
Dwell less in the past
Be less worried about the future
Be more motivated and inspired
Truly connect with others

...and much, much more! (Find out yourself.)

1.2 About us

Dr. Priscilla Schelp

Hi, I am Priscilla Schelp. I will guide you through the book and will involve Richard on many occasions. I am a start-up founder, manager, board member, researcher, moderator, keynote speaker, sailor, and polo enthusiast...and I love amazing people! I am Swiss-German and have worked and lived on different continents. Nowadays, I have an excellent global network that includes leaders in businesses, politics, diplomacy, NGOs, and science.

With my start-up networkx we do lead generation and prequalification for exclusive clubs around the world, such as private member, service, business, golf, polo, yacht, and art clubs. We aim to bring changemakers and visionaries into these networks to bring their visions to life! But I wasn't always this way. When I was in kindergarten, I was very artsy, often living in my own thoughts. Because of this, I grew up with kids bullying me and not leaving me alone. There was this constant desire to figure out what it takes to be a great person and connect well with people. So, during high school, I started reading. I had always loved reading, but I switched from my beloved books about horses to short articles such as: "How to Influence People" and the "Top 10 Tips on How to Make People Comfortable." What made me successful was not the simple act of reading, but rather that I always picked out one aspect that felt most appealing to me and practiced it until I mastered it before applying the next one. I trained and tested what worked for me!

I recommend you use this book the same way: read, test, train, revisit, and so on. You are never done with learning how to network or connect with people. If you build connections with people, you need to maintain and nurture those relationships. You cannot own plants, never water them and expect them to be alive and pretty, can you? They need water and sun, everything that allows them to grow, just like your relationships. The good thing is that if you apply the exercises in this book, connecting with people will become your number one hobby and transform your life!

Richard Lee-Thai

Now let me introduce you to my co-author, Richard Lee-Thai! He is a TEDx Speaker who delivered a talk entitled "How to Find Excuses to Connect," which outlines how people can make meaningful connections easier. There are many examples of human connection, storytelling, and community-building initiatives, but what they all have in common is finding an excuse to connect. Richard shows how anyone can apply these principles to find their own excuses to connect by distilling these examples into four core principles. He envisions a world where the term "excuse to connect" becomes part of our common vocabulary.

Richard is also the Founder of Excuses to Connect, a business focused on building connections through one-on-one coaching, podcasting, public speaking and merchandise. As a Connection Coach, he supports individuals and organizations in building their social confidence and fostering communities where everyone feels like they belong. His philosophy on life is captured in my motto: „You never know how any connection can transform your life." His ultimate vision is to empower and connect Connectors; together, we can transform our lives and the lives of others, one connection at a time.

1.2 How Richard and I met

So, how did we meet? Richard and I actually met on his Excuses to Connect podcast when he interviewed me for an episode. I found his podcast "Excuses to Connect," and the topic totally resonated with me. I felt compelled to reach out to him. Now we are writing a book together. See what can happen if you go out there and be open to new connections?

Connections can be life-changing, though they can seem difficult. The opposite of having meaningful connections is loneliness. This epidemic of loneliness plagues many people. We both know how it feels to be lonely, to feel rejected, and to struggle to connect with other people. We found a way to change that. We want to teach as many people as possible about what we have learned. We are certainly not the only people working within this realm of loneliness interventions and making connections, but we aim to add our personal experiences to this ongoing conversation.

Richard and I could not be more different. We grew up and lived on different continents and led different lives, but we share a common passion: We love connecting with people, AND we are not naturals. You know who you should take advice from? People that have gotten to where you want to be! Why should you listen to Richard and I? We are living examples that being good at connecting with people is not genetic, but it is a skill you can learn. We would not call ourselves natural talents in connecting, but we learned, developed, and became super connectors. We are not like consultants that tell others how to run their company but have never successfully done it ourselves.

We can prove that we are successfully doing it. We do not say that to brag but to give you empowerment. No matter what stage you're in right now, anything and everything is possible. So let us guide you through this book, and always remember: We feel you! We have been there too!

1.3 Why is this book so important to us?

To be able to make authentic connections, you need to love yourself, so other people can love you. Additionally, if you are authentic and show your true self, people can get to know and love the real you!

I had a beautiful childhood until I went to kindergarten. The world in my head was more kind than the children around me, so I went to hide there. I did enjoy school. My understandable but harmful strategy was not to show weakness, do nothing wrong, never fail, and always achieve my goals. This strategy formed the foundation of my life. I am not perfect, and no one is. If you, like me in the past, walk through life always fearing your next mistake, the idea of not being perfect, or trying to prove your worthiness, let me stop you with a warning. While it might be able to get you far in life, it is so stressful and exhausting. It feels like that because you are in a carnival 365 days a year. Don't get me wrong, the carnival is fun for a day, but never being allowed to be you, always being scared to fall out of character because you are scared that people could see who you really are, does that really sound fun? I don't know anyone who'd find that fun. You might think people cannot dislike you if you do not give them a reason to do so. Let me tell you something, they also can't really love you!

Why would you hide all these parts of yourself, the good and the bad? You hide them because you do not accept, do not like, and do not approve of these parts. You are saying NO to yourself. By hiding parts of yourself, you are reducing your authenticity and depth. It is like you are taking yourself from 3D to 2D. You are transferring reality to a scripted movie (which is exactly the definition of NOT being authentic). Even though we all like to watch a nice, pleasant movie, it will not really keep us hooked. We all want something and someone real!! We want to be real and loved exactly for that!

I had this awakening a few years ago when I was at university. We had to do some exercises from the career center. We were requested to write down our main skills and then asked friends and classmates what makes us special. I was quite surprised that nearly everyone I asked highlighted the same characteristic: assertiveness. One dear friend said, "Priscilla, I have never met anyone as determined as you are. If you want something and there is an obstacle, you find a way. You go over it, under it, around it, or through it. It does not matter; you find a way." I kind of had images of the series "White Collar" in my head, where the main character finds a very cool way to break out of prison. Sarcastically, I thought, "Great skills I have..."

Looking back, I realize that I have this skill because of my huge fear of being mediocre. I guess most of you understand me. In current times, being normal is not a compliment for most people, whereby, being special is something to strive for. Even though this fear brought me far, it also caused me much pain. I was so assertive because if I failed to achieve something, it would mean that I was not good enough or, worse, average. It got me far, but I paid a high price for it. I was constantly stressed. Now, I am not perfect, and still have some insecurities or worries sometimes. But overall, I know my worth, and I know I am good at what I do. My assertiveness is now fueled by my desire to learn and my wish to make a difference. If you have not realized your worth, this book will help.

Richard had similar feelings of inadequacy growing up. Due to being an only child, he dreaded summer, when he was alone with his thoughts and had few friends to spend time with. To cope, he conjured imaginary worlds and pretended to go on fun adventures. As he grew older, this sense of infrequent social interaction led to a fear of abandonment. He wanted close friends, so he would go out of his way to people-please and disregard his own boundaries. There was a constant sense of restlessness as he hustled to get external validation from others. He desperately wanted to hear from others that he was good enough and belonged. Even his parents placed high standards on him. To some extent, he was successful with this. He received many awards for his academic and extracurricular achievements but still felt hollow inside. The feelings of achievement would be temporary before he would set his mind on the next big thing he needed to do in order to feel worthy.

It wasn't until he started seeing a therapist during university that he was gradually able to uncover his self-limiting beliefs and behaviors. During his first session, his therapist gave the analogy that mental health is like a house. If the house is on fire, there's nothing else you can focus on except putting out the fire. However, if the house isn't on fire, there's an opportunity to renovate specific rooms. Richard wasn't seeking a mental health professional because he was in a crisis, but because he wanted to proactively take care of himself and renovate his house.

Over three years, he had cleaned out the dusty recesses of his house that he had never touched before. He realized his thought patterns of feeling like he was never good enough, and was gradually able to replace it with the belief that he was enough. He no longer needed to desperately seek validation from others through people-pleasing and trying to be perfect. He had become friends with himself. He fully accepted who he was and was able to treat himself with kindness. He felt grounded and it opened up the doors to more meaningful connections with others because he was already connected to himself.

When there was a leaky faucet in his metaphorical house, he was now equipped with tools to try to deal with the leak himself. When the issue was too big to handle, he knew that the wise decision would be to ask for help from a contractor. He had developed tools to be resilient and was comfortable asking for help when he needed it. By the end of therapy, he had a well-furnished, clean house.

It was not perfect, and maintenance still needed to be done, but it was in a much better condition.

He now had the tools and knowledge to help renovate other people's houses too. He wants to share his experiences within this book to help you better connect with yourself. To build a skyscraper, you need a strong and deeply-rooted foundation. This foundation is your relationship with yourself. We hope this book helps you with this.

I marked the chapters which Richard contributed mostly to with a *, so that you know and can give Richard credit for his valuable input ;)!

Now, let's get going!

Chapter 2 – Let's get Started

2.1 Let's start where you are!*

Chapter 2.1 to 2.4 are mostly written by Richard, who is definitely less emotional than me, so do not wonder ... Let's start with something interesting Richard told me:

Are you a noun or a verb? That may initially sound like a nonsensical question, but it profoundly affects how you view yourself and the world. A noun implies something is static, whereas a verb indicates an action. There is a difference between a human being and a human be-ing. The latter highlights that you are in a continual process of be-ing a human. It is active, living, and transformational.
I am Richard-ing. You are you-ing.

This linguistic distinction is important because it shifts you from being stuck as a noun and opens your mind to the possibility of change. In fact, change is always occur-ring. Who you are today is not the same person you were yesterday. Who you are tomorrow will not be the same person you are today. You have the capability of observing and influencing the type of person that you want to be. That is because you are a verb, not a noun.

This teaching comes from the Indigenous ways of know-ing. In Braiding Sweetgrass by Robin Wall Kimmerer talks about the grammar of animacy. Animacy refers to whether something (or someone) is alive. English is noun-based, whereas Robin's native language, Potawatomi, is more verb-based, consisting of 70% verbs.

In English, a hill is a noun. A beach is a noun. A bay of water is a noun. In Potawatomi, all of these are verbs: "to be a hill," "to be a long sandy stretch of beach," and "to be a bay." In other words, these are living, continual processes.

Robin goes on to explain that the word "it robs a person of selfhood and kinship, reducing a person to a mere thing... when we tell [our toddlers] that the tree is not a who, but an it, we make the maple an object; we put a barrier between us, absolving ourselves of moral responsibility and opening the door to exploitation... If a maple is an it, we can take up the chain saw. If the maple is a her, we think twice."

To stretch your mind even further, consider what diffe-rence it makes if you were to refer to yourself in third-person rather than first-person. For example, instead of saying, "I am Richard," let's explore, "Who is Richard? What relationship do I have with him? How do I want to relate to him?"

Let's do a little test! Most importantly, whatever the result is, there is no right or wrong. This is just for exploration! From wherever you sit or lie, get up and go to a mirror. Stand in front of it and look at yourself. Observe your thoughts. What are you thinking or saying to your-self? Are these nice thoughts, appreciation for yourself, or gratitude? Do you find yourself beautiful, or are you criticizing and shaming yourself for not being pretty, slim, trained...not good enough?

Are you finding yourself awesome, not just superficially, but you are accepting and loving yourself the way you are? Be honest: Are you having an extraordinary day, or is it a constant status? If yes, I am really happy for you! That is amazing that you are happy with yourself and love yourself. If you look at yourself with more critical eyes, you are not alone. Like you, most of us walk around the world, feeling not good enough in some way. You want to be loved just the way you are, so you go out in the world looking for a partner or friends that do that. But it is your job. No one can give you the love you are craving apart from you. You have to do that. You are then whole by yourself, and you can truly love others. Another advantage is that you need less approval and are less scared of rejection because you are not rejecting yourself. That's where the most beautiful connections grow.

After looking at your results, you now have a feeling of where you are and you can take it from there! You might want to try that test in between, at the end of the book, and occasionally to track your progress!

The rest of the book is structured to help you build everything you need brick by brick. Let's get started with learning how to connect with yourself.

2.2 Key question: What is possible?*

Imagine yourself as the seed of a plant. Over time, filaments of roots pop out of the seed and begin to draw nutrients from the surrounding soil. Under the right conditions, the seed sprouts its first leaf from out of the soil and interacts with the world above ground. This is not too far from reality.

You are not starting from scratch. Wherever you go, there you are. This is also the title of a book by Jon Kabat-Zinn, professor, and creator of the Stress Reduction Clinic and the Center for Mindfulness in Medicine. This means, however you got to where you are today, the past does not pre-determine your future! You are where you are today, and that is okay. You cannot change your past experiences, but ask yourself: Who do you want to be? Where do you want to go? What is possible?

What becomes possible if you are to let go of your self-limiting beliefs? What becomes possible if you are to surround yourself with people who are more aligned with you? What becomes possible if you truly believe that you are a confident connector?
Asking yourself, "What is possible?" is like planting a seed. Rather than thinking it is impossible, you are using your imaginative mind to envision possibilities, even if you don't fully believe in them at the moment. I'm not asking you to believe in it right now, I'm asking you to imagine: What if?

This book will help you continue nurturing that seed that you have just planted until it sprouts into a fully-fledged belief. Let's dig into it!

2.3 Nature vs. Nurture*

While it is true that nature shapes who you are, it is also important to understand nurture. For better or worse, you absorb the messaging from your environment and experiences. It shapes your beliefs and, consequently, how you feel and behave!

Brené Brown, a prominent researcher on shame and vulnerability, talks about a "culture of scarcity" in her book Daring Greatly. She says: "Scarcity is the 'never enough' problem. The word scarce is from the Old Norman French scars, meaning 'restricted in quantity' (c. 1300). Scarcity thrives in a culture where everyone is hyperaware of lack. Everything from safety and love to money and resources feels restricted or lacking. We spend inordinate amounts of time calculating how much we have, want, and don't have, and how much everyone else has, needs, and wants."

EXERCISE: Fill in the blank: I'm never _____ enough. Never good enough. Never perfect enough. Never beautiful enough. Never powerful enough. Never successful enough. Never smart enough. Never charismatic enough. Never funny enough. Never special enough. Now you know where your perceived weaknesses lie. This cultural ethos of lack instills this sense of needing to always be better or to obtain more to be happy.

The powerful thing to realize is that this is all due to nurture, not nature. This means that it is something you learned over time through societal messaging, and because it is something you learned, it can be unlearned. The belief that you just accept the situation is not as permanent as you think. Once you have a greater awareness of your thoughts, you will have the opportunity to gradually reprogram your beliefs in a way that serves you rather than holding you back.

How aware are you of your inner dialogue? I found this poignant example called the "Baby Picture Project," created by La Botanica Productions. In this short video, 12 people were asked about their deepest insecurities. They were asked to write down what the inner voice was always telling them. Then they were asked to say those negative thoughts to a picture of their younger selves. People stopped in their tracks. They started tearing up and hesitated.

One woman remarked: "I have to say these to her?"
To which the producer responded: "You say them to yourself."
Slowly, people started verbalizing their negative thoughts to their younger selves: "You're mediocre."
"You're not good enough."
"You're faking it, and everyone barely believes the lie."
"People don't like you."

They realized that they would never say these things about other people and make them feel this way, but at the same time, they were saying these things to themselves. Why were they so hard on themselves?

If self-criticism can be such a destructive behavior, why is it so prevalent? Why do our brains do this?
Kristin Neff, an expert on self-compassion, provides some answers to this question in her book Self-Compassion: The Proven Power of Being Kind to Yourself. These include biological factors, internalizing criticism from others, cultural messaging, and using it as a form of control.

As social creatures, we depend on being part of a community for our survival. Kristen points out that by criticizing ourselves in the presence of others, it can garner sympathy. Even when we position ourselves at the bottom of the pecking order by being self-deprecating, we can still remain a part of the pack.

Growing up, Richard was pressured by his parents to achieve high grades, and he was criticized when these standards weren't met. He had internalized this by believing that he had to be perfect in order to be enough. It's easy for external narratives to become ingrained, especially because children are like sponges. Even when he wasn't around his parents, he unconsciously repeated those same criticisms to himself. Kristen explains that criticisms from other people are blunted when it is simply something that you've said to yourself already.

Cultural messaging that stresses the ethic of independence, individual achievement, and self-criticism as a motivator, means that if we don't reach our ideal goals, we feel that we only have ourselves to blame. However, research found that self-criticism was strongly related to depression and dissatisfaction with life. While using self-criticism as a motivator works to some extent, a serious drawback is that anxiety becomes ingrained. The anxiety can undermine performance, whether with public speaking, tests, or stage fright. It is not emotionally neutral and places enormous pressure on trying to achieve to feel any sense of worthiness.

Lastly, self-criticism implies that self-control is possible, and that failure is something that can and should be avoided. Therefore, we have a desire to try to control situations, but ultimately, life is too unpredictable and complicated for us to fully control. This is evidenced by major events such as the COVID-19 pandemic, which resulted in major disruptions to the economy, healthcare system and how we interact. However, it would not be self-compassionate to call ourselves failures and blame ourselves when the external circumstances weren't really within our control.

Kristen encapsulates the trap of self-criticism when she says: "If self-criticism works at all, however, it is only for one reason: fear. Because it is so unpleasant to be harshly criticized by ourselves when we fail, we become motivated by the desire to escape our own self-judgment."

Given all these biopsychosocial factors that contribute to people being self-critical, we can offer ourselves some forgiveness. We are conditioned through our environment to be self-critical because it's a coping mechanism. However, if we want to reprogram the way we talk to ourselves, the best way is to understand it and replace it with a kinder response. Trying to beat ourselves up for being self-critical is like adding fuel to the fire. The goal is to douse the fire with water.

Self-compassion allows us to hold ourselves with kindness and recognize that our struggles are part of the human experience and that negative emotions can be approached mindfully. This possibility is accessible by anyone, regardless of how you were nurtured.

2.4 Introversion vs. Extraversion*

Would you consider yourself an introvert, extrovert, or ambivert? Wherever you are on the spectrum, you can still confidently connect with people. It's a myth that introverts are shy and awkward. As an introvert myself, I describe introversion as using up my energy when I'm in social situations and needing alone time to recharge. I am more drawn to solitary activities such as journaling and meditation. I also prefer one-on-one conversations instead of being in loud spaces with many people. I don't crave being the center of attention, and I'm not the life of the party, but I am comfortable with public speaking and taking on leadership roles.

In Susan Cain's book Quiet: The Power of Introverts in a World that Can't Stop Talking, she outlines how society tends to value extraversion above introversion, and it's reflected in the way that our institutions are designed. For example, Cain shares the prevalence of team-based work and open-design office spaces that are meant to create more collaboration. However, introverts might prefer having their own quiet space where they focus on their work, rather than needing to socialize.

Susan is not anti-extraversion. Instead, she is advocating for a world where introverts and extroverts are mutually respected and valued for the skills and perspective they bring to the world. Introversion and extraversion are just one dimension that helps you to better understand yourself, but the labels shouldn't box you in. There is such a thing as a sociable introvert and a shy extrovert.

As an introvert, Richard was often criticized for being "too quiet" as a kid. He thought it was a bad thing to be quiet. People thought that being quiet meant being shy. But now he knows that being quiet means he is listening, and it's one of his strengths. "Speak in such a way that others love to listen to you. Listen in such a way that others love to speak to you;" this is from the American author Zig Ziglar. Richard loves this quote because it highlights how communication is not just about speaking, but also about listening.

In case I did not mention, I was always on the introvert side when doing any tests, just in the recent year, I am slightly more on the extravert side. So, it seems you can slightly adjust...

If you're still unsure where you fall on the introvert-extrovert spectrum, a self-assessment is included below. Answer each question "true" or "false," choosing the answer that applies to you more often than not.

1. I prefer one-on-one conversations to group activities.
2. I am more likely to recharge my batteries by getting some alone time, rather than going out with a group of friends.
3. I don't like being the center of attention.
4. I seem to care less than my peers about wealth, fame, and status.
5. Dislike small talk, but I enjoy talking in depth about to pics that matter to me.
6. When I meet someone for the first time, I usually do most of the listening.
7. I tend to be reserved when dealing with people I don't know well.
8. At social events, I rarely try to introduce myself to new people and mostly talk to the ones I already know.
9. I feel more drawn to places that are quiet and intimate rather than busy and bustling.
10. The people who know me best would describe me as quiet and reflective.
11. In general, I am more likely to feel overwhelmed and overstimulated than bored and under-stimulated.
12. I dislike conflict.
13. I would love a job that required me to work alone most of the time.
14. I tend to be quiet and observant in group conversations, rather than feeling the need to speak up.
15. I feel drained after being out and about, even if
16. I've enjoyed myself.
17. I'm a private person.
18. In my free time on the weekend, I'd prefer sharing a deep conversation with a good friend rather than mingling at a party with people I've never met before.

19. I prefer a few deep, close relationships, instead of many casual ones.
20. I look at life from the inside out.
21. In classroom situations, I prefer lectures to seminars.

The more often you answered "true," the more introverted you probably are. If you found a roughly equal number of "true" and "false" answers, you may be an ambivert.

Even though the whole focus of my work is on the topic of connection, you would most likely see me being quiet and observing when in a group setting. I don't crave being the center of attention, and I'm not the life of the party. However, that doesn't mean I'm shy or somehow incapable of making meaningful connections with people. It just means I have a preferred manner of interacting.

Richard is great friends with people who are extraverts. He even has a friend who prides herself as someone who is "99% extraverted!" She brings charismatic energy to a room, and she's energized by groups of people. Richard once interviewed an extrovert on his podcast who described his ideal day as having eight meetings because he feels energized through all those interactions. Though Richard finds it interesting, the idea feels exhausting for him as an introvert.

If you want to delve deeper into understanding your own personality type, there is also the Big Five Personality Assessment that you can take: https://www.truity.com/test/big-five-personality-test. This is also known as the OCEAN model, because it assesses people on Openness, Conscientiousness, Extraversion, Agreeableness, and Neuroticism. The purpose of this is not to box people into a certain label, but to provide insight into your tendencies.

2.5 Everything is Possible

I believe that everything is possible. My dear co-author, Richard, and I are both living examples that you do not have to be born a certain way to become a super networker. Both of us were introvert, and not particularly sociable growing up, nor did we come from super well-connected families. But we made it, and so can you. You can create everything you want yourself. You want to create a world-class network yourself? No problem!

Are there factors that might make it easier or quicker to build up a world-class network? For sure! It helps to be beautiful, smart, or have a family that can help you build your network.

But do you know what the good news is? In the end, people connect with your personality and your soul. Modern technology makes it easier than ever to connect with people, even around the world. No matter where you are now, how far you are now or how old you are, it is not too late! At the beginning of this chapter, you assessed your status quo.

Let's get started from this moment. Each moment is always passing and changing. This current moment is like a snapshot—it is not who you are. You are just capturing a situation at a point in time. It is not who you permanently are.

2.6 The Superself Framework

Richard and I developed a three-part framework to help you have the best possible relationship with yourself. The framework is an iterative cycle. First, you need to accept yourself, take care of yourself, and develop yourself. When you are done with one iteration, you've got your new self to continue accepting, taking care of, and developing.

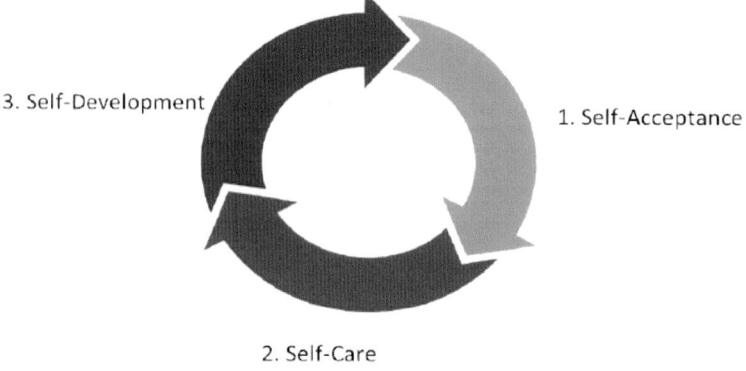

3. Self-Development

1. Self-Acceptance

2. Self-Care

Figure 1 Superself Framework

The next three chapters provide you with practical guidance on how to master each framework component!

Chapter 3 – Self-Acceptance*

3.1 How much do you accept and love yourself? A quick test.

Before you can genuinely connect with others, you need to connect with yourself. This means that you need to love yourself first. But most importantly, you need to make yourself happy.

Imagine your happiness being a key made of glass. Imagine your partner or best friend giving you his/her glass key and telling you, "You are now responsible for this key being shiny and whole for the rest of my life." While you might feel flattered by the gesture, you will probably not feel comfortable. Instead, you'll feel pressured by this huge responsibility. You'll be asking yourself, "Can I actually do this?" That's how you make people feel if you place your happiness in their hands.

So the ideal scenario where you can build up a real connection is when you are happy with yourself and the other person is happy with themselves, allowing you to embrace each other. You do not need each other. People sense neediness, and it makes you less attractive to them.

> Kahlil Gibran's poem On Marriage seems to capture this ideal beautifully:
>
> "Let there be spaces in your togetherness.
> And let the winds of the heavens dance between you.
> Love one another but make not a bond of love:

Let it rather be a moving sea between the shores of your souls.
Fill each other's cup but drink not from one cup.
Give one another of your bread but eat not from the same loaf.
Sing and dance together and be joyous, but let each one of you be alone,
Even as the strings of a lute are alone though they quiver with the same music.
Give your hearts, but not into each other's keeping.
For only the hand of Life can contain your hearts.
And stand together, yet not too near together:
For the pillars of the temple stand apart,
And the oak tree and the cypress grow not in each ot her's shadow."

This chapter is about the inner work you must do to build a proper foundation.

EXERCISE: This exercise is called the eye gazing exercise and is from I am Enough: Mark Your Mirror and Change Your Life by Marissa Peer. Go in front of a mirror, and look into your eyes. Choose one eye to focus on. Tell yourself, "I love you," and notice and document how you react/feel. If you feel overwhelmed by pain or even have tears, this is not unusual; it is rather an indication that you are currently not loving yourself enough.

3.2 Inner world vs. Outer world

In a nutshell, we have an inner and outer world. The inner world is what you think and feel and what happens inside you. The outer world is what happens around you.

Let's assume you are talking to a colleague today, and she is very rude to you. There are various ways how you could interpret it. She might have had a horrible day? But because you don't know everything about her or her day, you might assume she never liked you or has it out to get you. See, something happens in the outer world, and you interpret it. How you interpret such an event depends very much on previous personal experiences, what you believe about you, other people, and the world. Most times, when a person has a bad reaction, most times it's not about them and not you. However, most of us take situations like the described one personally and it hurts us. It is important for us to realize that things happening in the outer world cannot hurt us. The only thing that can hurt us is how we interpret what happens.

Did you notice that when you feel bad (if that is not bad enough), additionally everything on that day goes wrong? The other way, if you feel amazing, all kinds of good things happen around you!? There are different reasons for that. If you are positive, you focus more on the positive and the other way around. Additionally, other people feel your positive energy and vibes. You behave like a winner, more positive and confident. And people are more likely to want to have you around! Or do you particularly enjoy it if you go to a shop with grumpy personnel, for example?

Generally, if bad things happen to you all the time, you likely have bad stuff going on in your head. You have beliefs that are not serving you. Generally, the quality of your thoughts determines the quality of your life! Create a nice surrounding in your head, and you will find your life getting more and more bright. It means that you need to start from the inner world. Most people do the opposite; they go to the gym, do diets, work hard, and date new partners, and it just does not work out well for them. Why? Because their beliefs are e.g., "I am not loveable." If you put that in your brain, your brain will go out and find evidence for that and achieve that goal of you being not loved. That's why, even if you do things like go out and meet people, you will not end up with a happy dating life, because you will self-sabotage!

3.3 What do you believe about yourself?

We all have many beliefs. A belief is something you tell yourself about yourself, others, or the world that you accept as true.

A lot of these were formed in our childhood. For example, your parents might have told you that you are sporty but not orderly. Generally, a belief itself is neither good nor bad by nature. However, it is important that you know which beliefs you have to assess if they serve you. You can distinguish by asking yourself how the belief makes you feel and if it brings you closer or further away from who you want to be and the life you want to have.

I generally have the belief that everything is possible, for everyone. For many people, negative beliefs are the main restriction to living the life they want. Examples of negative beliefs are: "In the end, we are all on our own," "I am not good with people," "I am shy," or a classic, "I am not good enough." Why are these bad for you? Because they keep you from connecting with yourself and other people. I am confident that you are or at least can become good at connecting with people. And not just that: You can also become good at connecting other people with each other! I believe one of the best ways to be successful in life is to help others succeed.

So let's analyze how these negative beliefs actually harm

you. I will give you some examples from my own life. One of the main negative beliefs I struggled with in the past was not feeling good enough. I continuously needed to get approval, compliments, and achievements to feel good enough. When I was sick and unable to work, I lacked that approval and sense of achievement; I felt horrible and unworthy. When in a relationship, I needed to hear compliments and get attention. Otherwise, I would question whether my partner still loves me. If I went to an event, I would not focus on all the cool people who liked me but on the ones who seemed not to like me.

Do you believe that you are a good person? Do you believe you are special? Do you believe you can achieve anything? I believe you can! I believe we are all able to achieve great things. I believe most of us have nearly unlimited potential, and you do too!

The world would have fewer problems, wars, and crime if everyone was self-confident and happy with themselves. Most people are not, and most of the time, it is due to the negative beliefs they hold about themselves. This is also probably one of the key things from you having the network and the relationships you desire.

How many of these boundaries do you have?

EXERCISE: List your positive and negative beliefs in a two-column list. List what you believe is loveable about you. What do you not love about yourself? What do you believe you are good or bad at?

EXERCISE: Take the negative beliefs and replace these with more positive ones.

There are two main ways how you can implement beliefs in the way they work:

1. Replace a belief about you e.g., "I am not good enough," with "I am good enough."

You need two things to ensure it works: 1. Phrase the belief as it applies to you as you are right now. Vishen Lakhiani believes that beliefs are just accepted by your brain when your brain believes that it is who you are right now. Therefore, "I will be good enough" will not work; and 2. You really need to take a belief as though it is true for you right now, if not, your brain will reject it, and it could even make you feel worse, because you feel like
you are lying to yourself. In that case, you might not turn from "I am ugly" to "I am beautiful," but choose a step in between. For example, you can say, "I look OK," and you can level up once you feel comfortable with this belief. I do not suggest the use of negation in beliefs as our brains do not understand it well. Why should you not use negation in beliefs, in goal setting, or anything else. By defining what you do not want, you do not define what you want. Therefore, your brain takes on the information you give it and deletes the "not." That's why people who say that they do not want to date a lazy person, end up with exactly that.

2. Replace "I am not sporty" with "I commit to going to the gym three times a week."

If you struggle with making the first type of belief adjustment, choose a belief where you do not change what you believe about yourself, but commit to an action that brings you closer to the belief you want to have. This is an alternative belief adjustment method developed by Dr. Srikumar Rao.

To make the most of this exercise, look at your positive

beliefs regularly, every day, if you can. Review them regularly and raise the bar.

Not only will you be happier as your beliefs get better, but it will also increase your confidence.

3.4 Are you really alone?*

"The only thing keeping you from being happy is the belief that you are alone." – Anna Draper. There is no doubt that loneliness is a painful experience. In the book Atlas of the Heart by Brené Brown, she explains that current neuroscience research shows that the pain of loneliness triggers the same regions of our brain as if we were experiencing physical pain. However, believing that we are alone in our experiences amplifies this feeling of loneliness.

Do you relate to any of the following statements?
>   I am afraid of rejection.
>   I am afraid of not knowing what to say.
>   I am afraid that I am bothering other people.
>   I am afraid of missing out.
>   I am afraid of being lonely.

Richard asked this question during a workshop he was conducting, and the attendees unanimously said they related to all the statements. This surprised the attendees, as they realized that their private, internal concerns were also shared by everyone else. There is a stigma when it comes to expressing our fears and loneliness. However, the more it is talked about, the more it is normalized. The more it is normalized, the less shame there is because it is seen as simply part of the collective human experience.

You might still be thinking: "That's great and all, but I don't know anyone personally to relate to what you're describing."

This is a fair point and highlights the gap between intellectual and emotional understanding. During a 4-day Indigenous Relations Program, one of the facilitators said: "The shortest and longest distance is from the mind to the heart." Physically, the distance between one's brain and heart isn't that far, but metaphorically, there's a large distance between knowing something with your mind versus knowing with your heart.

When Richard moved away to a new city, he had to start from scratch. He didn't know anyone there, and struggled with loneliness during his first year at that university. Richard knew intellectually that he wasn't the only person going through this, but there wasn't anyone specific he could point to. It wasn't until Richard started his Humans of ULeth project that he interviewed students and professors, and shared their stories online.

When Richard asked them about their first-year experience, he could relate to the stories they were sharing of moving from other cities and struggling to make friends in a foreign environment. He was now able to say, "Victoria went through the same thing as me." Richard bridged the gap between an intellectual understanding to an emotional, experiential understanding.

When you think back to the question, "Are you really alone?" if the answer is yes, it may be because of the gap between a mind-centered versus a heart-centered understanding.

3.5 Why You Really Failed and the Snapshot

I was on the athletics team when I was a kid in school. I was fairly good at running and jumping disciplines. But on the other side, if I had to do anything involving my arms like throwing a ball or javelin, I wasn't great at it. In my favorite discipline, "high jumping," I got very good but I struggled because I hit a glass ceiling. Our trainer always told us the height of the bar before we jumped, so whenever the bar was at 1.35m, I failed. I believed I'd never succeed and started to feel a sense of doubt just trying. One day, when I was about to jump, our trainer told me it was 1.35m. After I made the successful jump, he said with delight, "Priscilla, you just jumped 1.40m." It was then that it really hit me. It was never that I couldn't jump that height, but rather, I'd sabotaged my brain into thinking I couldn't. Now, I can tell you numerous examples in my life that somewhat went in that same direction.

Actually, most times in life, when I failed, it was not because I was not good enough, but because I THOUGHT I was not good enough. That is very sad. On the one hand, we cannot change the past and must make peace with it. However, if you are aware of that bias, it offers you so much potential in the future! You can do almost everything; you just need to believe in it.

EXERCISE: List three times when you failed big? Be honest with yourself. Did you really fail because you were not good enough? Or was it your head telling you so? When you decide to jump, don't let your mind fool you into thinking you can't.

3.6 The Power of Focus

Why is your mindset so important? A lot of things happen in your mind, and depending on how you think, you win or lose. If you think you will win, you will. If you think you will fail, you will. The mind is a beautiful thing. It is like a supercomputer that serves us. Our brain will aim to get us what we program it to do, which can ultimately be powerful!

During the COVID-19 pandemic, I could not sail, so I decided I wanted to learn to play polo. Now, polo is generally considered a very challenging and dangerous sport. You play polo on horses at high speed with so-called mallets, a small ball, and lots of protective gear. I am, by nature, one of those people who is scared of everything, which does not make it easier.

Additionally, since birth, I have not been able to see three-dimensionally. In school, I was always elected last in sports teams if the discipline had anything to do with balls. Imagine someone like me being on a horse at full speed, hitting a tiny ball. Well, this did not stop me. I wanted to learn so badly that I took polo and additional riding lessons. I did not stop there. I got a special training plan for the gym (six times a week) to build the required muscles. During my lunch breaks, I would train the swings with a walking stick (a shorter mallet with which you can train the swings without a horse). I am still no pro, but I did it. Isn't that encouraging? If you really want something, a lot is possible!

Well, I also often applied the power of focus the other way around, and I am not proud of it. The power of focus can serve you if you focus on something positive. If you focus on what you do not want or your fears, you can sabotage yourself. And doing that has already cost me a lot. It nearly cost me my PhD:

Due to lack of data availability in my PhD, I had to switch from a qualitative to a quantitative approach. I never had problems with math or statistics; however, I did not have to use it much in my work or university setting, so I was worried if I could achieve a quants doctorate. I ended up receiving good support from my supervisors and statisticians. I was doing well.

However, I had several occasions where I got stuck and thought I could not do it. My supervisors and statisticians were convinced I could and tried to convince me. They were not successful. I was stubborn like a donkey. I was not moving. I was so focused on the thought that I could not do it, why I couldn't, and which skills and knowledge I was missing. There were two to three occasions in the last two years of my doctorate where I really drove the people around me nuts and was about to quit my PhD even though I was already very close to completion.

Let me ask you: Be honest, have you ever been in a relationship with a person, and you really loved the person and wanted to be with him or her, but you messed it up because you were too scared?

Our mind is like a Google search. Let's imagine you enter into the Google search engine a conspiracy or exaggerations e.g., that Elon Musk has 30 children or that Bill Gates started Corona (I just made these up). There is nothing that does not exist, so you will probably have some Google hits, but does it mean that these rumors are true? No! So, basically, even if you have beliefs that do not serve you and these are not true, your brain will find evidence. You believe people do not like you if you meet them the first time; you will find evidence for it!

Getting back to the relationship example: Even though you want to be with the person, you are so scared that the person might not love you anymore, that instead of appreciating the love the other person shows you, you are not seeing it because you are busy looking for clues why the other person does not love you. And guess what: In that moment, your goal is not to be in a relationship, your goal is your fear. You are messing the relationship up yourself.

What you focus on expands! And the direction you choose is where you go. If you are in the car and looking right, that's where you will drive (don't try). Let's test this hypothesis in a less dangerous way!

EXERCISE: List what went wrong today and then list what went well.

When you focus on writing down what went wrong today, there are probably many things you can think of. Now, when you focus on the opposite, what went well, you can probably also think of plenty of things. Now that you see that focus has such a big impact, you might want to train that—we will get into that in a bit. What is very important here is that you do not beat yourself up for having negative beliefs or thoughts. Your negative beliefs mainly developed due to your environment or events. Negative thoughts happen. Generally, now that you can see how powerful your brain is, be kind and see your brain as your friend. It tries to protect you. But like a dog that thinks that it is protecting you when it is biting the mailman, your brain might be overprotective of you, due to past pain. So we will teach you tips and tricks to move your mindset in the right direction or get it back when you are drifting.

Here is one more example where you can see how much focus can impact you and your life. Do you know people that dwell in the past? People who dwell in the past become sad and depressed, because the past is gone. In the same way, people thinking about the future worry because they do not know what is coming. It makes them anxious. Having a vision for the future is good, but you should focus on the present!

There are some tools that can help you to feel happy such as meditation, journaling, gratitude, spending time in nature, sports, helping someone, etc. but also connecting with people.

EXERCISE: My tip: To maintain your focus, write a journal daily; this will also help you with other topics we will cover. I am not talking about a romantic "Dear Diary..." (you can do that too if you prefer), but I am talking about writing down three things you love about yourself each day. You have an example of my journey structure at the end of the book.

3.7 Telling yourself what you've always been waiting to hear from others

The less dependent you are on external validation, the more stable you will be emotionally. If you know you can give everything you need to yourself, you will not be yearning and waiting for someone else to provide it to you. This one is a lesson I learned quite late. For a long time, I wanted to excel, have good grades, do good at work, and look good so that other people tell me that I am pretty, lovable, smart, and so on. This yearning for someone else's approval really caused me so much damage in the past. It is like handing the key to your happiness to someone else. I spent so much time and effort to get loved and accepted by other people that did not see my value. I learned that just because someone does not see your value does not mean you have no value. I did nice things or was nice and expected people to return the favor; if not, I would resent them. If people, especially partners, would not often tell me how they appreciate me and give me compliments, I would feel unsettled. I spent countless hours trying to guess what other people think and why they do certain things (to me). It cost me my peace. It took time for me to understand that you cannot control other people, and most likely, for many people, you are not the centre of their universe. Additionally, in some countries, like Germany, people tend to be less expressive regarding compliments and emotional statements. Being dependent on other people's validation is an Achilles heel. It can make you fall. If you are dependent on other people, you are easy to manipulate, and your own emotions can easily derail you.

During a short meditation retreat, the teacher led us through a powerful exercise. We were asked to think about a phrase we've always wanted to hear someone say to us, but we haven't received often or at all. For me, it was along the lines of: "I am proud of everything you are and do." We were to visualize who we wanted to say that to us, like we were in the same room as them.

Now, we were asked to say that phrase to ourselves. We could provide it to ourselves. We didn't need to wait for someone else to do it for us. As I told myself what I'd always wanted to hear, I started to tear up. All this time, I thought I needed everyone else—their acceptance and love, when I could have provided that to myself the whole time. It ultimately came down to giving myself acceptance in order to heal the insecurities that I had internalized.

EXERCISE: Write down at least three things you love about yourself and your three wins in your journal daily.

What you love about yourself can be something you love about your body, some qualities you have, the way you dress, it can be anything. Regarding your three wins of the day, these can be things you achieved, fears you faced, a way you improved your life, that you helped someone else, etc. If you want to intensify the effect of the exercise, you can take your journal, stand in front of a mirror, look into your eyes and tell yourself what you love about yourself and what you are proud of. You might tell yourself that you love yourself and that you are enough at the end of the exercise. It forces you to look more within yourself and not outside of yourself.

Now that you have the knowledge and tools that help you to accept yourself, we will provide you with insights and exercises to take care of yourself.

Chapter 4 – Self-Care

4.1 Victim vs. Growth mindset

A victim mindset is where you perceive that bad things happen around you all the time, you are unlucky, things go wrong, and it is never your fault. You poor thing!! These happen due to external circumstances or other people—you think! But you are wrong!

I met quite a few people like that in my life. When I was doing my doctorate, there was one lady like that in my course. She was an interesting person and likable. But there was always drama in her life. I was frequently wondering why so many bad things kept happening to her.

One PhD colleague of mine once said one smart thing: If things happen to you repeatedly, it is a pattern. And do you know what the patterns have in common? The person it is happening to. Now, observing these kinds of people, you see that they create drama around them. Typically, it is because they have a belief that does not serve them.

A former successful and good-looking friend was always in lawsuits with people. He always assumed people would betray him. The bad thing is that people tend to show you what you expect from them. That's why I advise you always to expect the best from people. People do not like to disappoint and will try to live up to your standards.

Why is the victim mindset so bad? And yes, other peo-ple suffer from you blaming them and from you complain-ing all the time. But the person that suffers most is you, you alone! Whatever happens around you or to you and whoever's "fault" it is, you need to take accountability. In most cases, you are not helpless, but you can take an active role, you can act, or at least you can change your interpretation of what happened. That's why I love the saying, "If you do not like it change it, if you cannot change it, change your mindset!" By taking accountability and taking on an active role, you will feel much more in control and less helpless.

If you can change it, change it. If you can't change it, change your mindset.

EXERCISE: Identify bad things or situations that happened/ happen to you repeatedly. Most likely, it is you that these occasions have in common. Identify the underlying belief that is creating these situations. Think about how you can replace them.

4.2 Big events will not change your life!

Most of us walk through life aiming for the big events such as meeting the love of our life, our summa cum laude graduation, our dream wedding, a dream vacation, our first child, dream job or promotion. Maybe even a lottery win to make our life richer in material things and happiness. This is in vast conflict with research results: If you measure the happiness of a person, you will notice that the effects of good events do not last longer than a couple of months or a year. What was an event you thought would change your life? How long did that good feeling last?

I know I felt like that a couple of times in my life! I felt amazing when I was accepted at KPMG and moved to Singapore! I thought my life would be fantastic from then on! Well, I got used to it quite quickly. You continue living your life and are waiting for the next big thing. Because you still believe there is something out there that can make you happy. You just think it was not the right thing—this very dangerous belief keeps you in this thought trap.

A person's happiness level is pretty stable over time. Every one of us has a baseline happiness. It is the general happiness level we are operating at and the level our happiness comes back to after recovering from good or bad events. The learning here is that instead of looking for the big fix or silver bullet for your happiness, you might want to focus on increasing your baseline happiness. We will provide you with insights and tools on how to do that later.

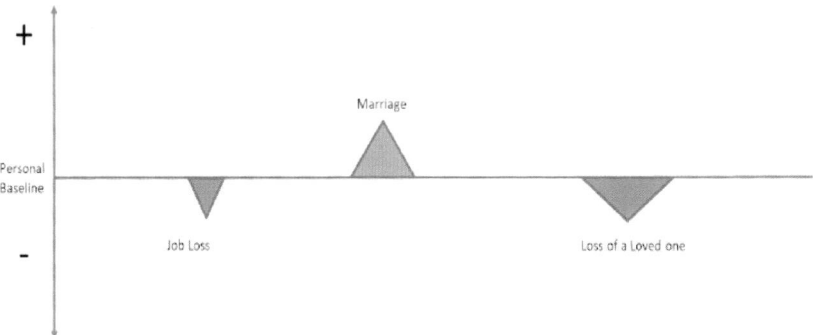

Figure 2 Simplified Baseline happiness over 10 years

We talked about the effects on our happiness that we expect from big, positive events or achievements. We have the same expectations contrarily as well. We expect that if we fail that exam or get fired from that job, our life will be ruined for a long time. We assume that our life is over if we lose our spouse or have a deadly disease like AIDS. Interestingly, a study showed that these negative effects on happiness last for around a year, and you return to your baseline happiness.

To sum it up, the expected strength and duration of the effect are much higher than the experienced effect. What does that mean? Instead of hoping for big events to change your life for the better, focus on improving your mindset and habits to improve your baseline happiness. Don't worry; it is not that hard. The good thing is that you do not have to look for the big things, but you can start right now.

EXERCISE: If you worry about a future event ruining your life, remind yourself that you expect the outcome to have a bigger impact than it will have in reality.

REMINDER: If you think the next big thing will fix your life. Remind yourself that it will just be for a short time, do not forget to work on your baseline happiness with the exercises in the upcoming sections.

4.3 The Power of Gratitude and Appreciation of Small Things

Gratitude has allowed me to appreciate ordinary magic more deeply. Gratitude allows me to appreciate what I have, rather than lamenting over the things that I don't have. The simple act of drinking water can truly be refreshing if I pay attention. Or just to look outside and watch the clouds. Things are constantly changing, some moments being extraordinarily ordinary, some bringing intense joy or pain, and everything in between. This is how my days go.

Treating challenging experiences with a bit more levity and expressing gratitude for all the gifts that are a part of my everyday life. The privilege of having access to a home, food, education, and technology. The gift of someone's time, an act of kindness like a hug, and a smile. A listening ear, a shoulder to cry on, and words of encouragement. Learning a bit more every day, building resiliency, and surfing the ups and downs of life.

Today is a microcosm of life, and we have the power of intention to guide how we move through it. Happiness might already be right here, rather than somewhere in the distant future or in a far-off place. How we live our days is how we live our lives.
You know what the most amazing thing about gratitude is: If you feel grateful, you cannot feel scared or depressed simultaneously. It prevents you from having negative feelings.

EXERCISE: Journaling. Write at least three things you are grateful for daily in your journal. I will provide more details on journaling later in the book.

EXERCISE: Mindfulness. Try to really use your senses on a daily basis. For example, smell your perfume, enjoy the breeze through your hair, and feel how your skin feels. You will automatically be in the moment.

4.4 You can Enhance Your State by Physical Change

Do you sometimes sit in a coffee shop and observe people? You can see from their posture and facial expression how they feel? Did you ever see someone slouching that was super energetic? Did you ever see someone super happy that was not smiling? Tony Robbins indicated that it is not just that your feelings create your posture and facial expressions, but the effect is also the other way around. If you take on a straight posture, move back your shoulders, relax your muscles, smile, and breathe calmly, you feel different automatically. Doing physical activity will also help you feel better. Thereby, you can change your mental state by changing your physical setting.

EXERCISE: First, we will help you relax, and then we will get you going!

Sit down comfortably with your eyes closed. The first time you breathe out slowly, relax your eyes and forehead. The next time you breathe out, relax your neck, shoulders, chest, and abdomen. Finally, take a deep breath and open your eyes. You've got this. You can do anything.
Stand up, pull your shoulders back, chin up and smile. My personal touch is that I have a certain victory gesture that I do at the end. You probably know this retro postcard where there is a woman with a dotted hairband that flexes her arm, and says, "We can do it." I have a gesture similar to that, but I make a fist, flex my arm, shake it, and shout, "Yes!" like I just won the lottery. I recommend you establish your own winning gesture. This gesture will make you smile, motivate you, and boost your energy.

4.5 You can Change Your Mental State

Another way to change your state is by mental power. Let us do an exercise together:

EXERCISE: Define the feeling/s you want to feel. In which situation did you feel that feeling strongly in the past? Close your eyes and visualize. Be in that situation: What did you see, feel, smell... Be in the situation; the more real, the better. Now, very important, recap how you felt, feel that feeling. Embrace it!

I recommend you define at least one feeling you want to

be able to feel. This exercise enables you (if you are familiar with it and have practiced it well) to access the feeling of pressing a button. If you want to feel two feelings in a situation, for example, you can do the exercise with one feeling first, then with the other.

Let me tell you which feelings I chose, why, and how they help me.

Meeting (new) People
I want to feel loved, inspired, and like everything is possible for me.
When I meet new people, I want them to feel the warmth of caring about them. Remember, I am naturally a shy person. Before I go to an event where I know I will meet many new people, I want to feel loved. Love pushes away fear and any negative feelings. It enables you to see the good new people you meet.

Doing Keynote Speeches or Being Interviewed
As a naturally shy person, I have stage fright. However, before I perform, I use this exercise to feel inspired, so I can inspire others. If you are excited about your vision and mission, there is no space for worrying about how other people perceive you.

Before Pitching to Customers, Partners, or Investors
I use this exercise to feel like everything is possible, so I don't self-sabotage the outcome. Especially when you persuade people, you need to be convinced that a positive outcome is possible and likely.

I recommend you use these methods for situations where you are currently struggling with limiting beliefs. Start thinking about which situations you find hard. Next, think about how you usually feel in these situations. Then think about how you want to feel instead and use this exercise to practice. This way, you can recap these situations easily and manage your state.

4.6 Your Words Matter

Imagine you are having a bad day. You started the day by spilling coffee all over your clothes and laptop. At least your laptop still works, and you can change your clothes because you sit in your home office. The first email you read is from your company's client, and it does not sound friendly. A major failure happened. You are supposed to do everything ASAP. To make matters worse, you did not sleep well, so you are growling. Your eyes are heavy, and you need to focus more than ever. You're wondering how you will get through this in one piece. Do you have days like that?

You might think to yourself, "Today is horrible." You might even think to yourself or tell a colleague or friend, "This is catastrophic." Well, even though most of us say things like that occasionally, just stop. You are not doing your-self any favors.

Remember the part about your brain being your friend and supercomputer? Your brain always listens and will auto-matically react to words like "catastrophe" or "disaster," so you are giving your brain alarm signals which will mas-sively increase your stress level. I agree; the above-de-scribed situation is not pleasant, but is it worth getting into emergency mode? Avoiding such wordings reduces the amount and frequency of emergencies for your brain. If you are in situations like that, instead of freaking out or going into emergency or victim mode (Why is that happening to me?), this exercise might help:

EXERCISE: If you are in a stressful situation, remind yourself not to use trigger words such as "disaster," "catastrophic," or "horrible."

Instead, in a stressful situation, affirm for yourself, "I can do that. I am good enough. I have everything inside me to handle this."

4.7 How to Handle Unpleasant Thoughts

A study in 2020 found that everyone of us has roughly 6000 thoughts per day. As you might know, not all of these thoughts are positive or pleasant. Some days, you might feel low and have much more negative than positive thoughts. You might feel like a bad person because of that! The good news: you are not your thoughts.

When you do have negative thoughts, do not blame yourself. There is nothing wrong with you. These thoughts are your normal internal protection mechanism. Your brain is your friend and tries to protect you the best it can. Always remember that.

I compare my brain with my favorite polo horse, Furia. Furia was calm and kind. I felt confident and in the lead. Furia knew exactly what to do. She accepted me as the leader. Yes, I phrased that in the past tense on purpose. After an accident that hurt my spine, I trained on Furia the first time, and everything went wrong. It was like I was sitting on a completely different polo pony. She was just doing what she wanted. What happened? She felt that I was scared, I was not being a leader anymore. She felt that to keep us safe, she had to take over. The same happens with your brain when you are scared, insecure, etc. You need to tame your horse, meaning, you have to tame your thoughts. Otherwise, they dictate you. I will show you an exercise on how to do that. One important point is that you just observe your thoughts. Do not judge yourself for having negative thoughts, do not take them as a reality or your thoughts being you, just observe. This exercise will help you with it!

EXERCISE: Imagine you are an eagle flying in the sky, your thoughts are the weather that see beyond you through the clouds. Now, below the clouds, there is a storm. You fly and fly, and there are fewer clouds. You fly further, and it is sunny weather. You can see all the streets and tiny houses and trees clearly, bringing you relief. The weather is our thoughts. The storms and rain are unpleasant thoughts. You want to have a bird's perspective and just let your thoughts pass by.

You are not your thoughts. Your thoughts are generated from your beliefs. If you have certain streams of unpleasant thoughts more often, write them down, think about which underlying belief could cause these, and exchange the belief with a more positive one.

4.8 Improve Your Well-being by Naming Your Emotions*

One of my best friends has a new girlfriend. My friend is super friendly, sympathetic, and very appreciative towards her. Well, she regularly snaps at him and acts quite aggressively. I was surprised. I observed the two and occasionally checked in with him. One day something clicked in my brain. I realized what was going on. She was suffering from a phenomenon I've seen far more with men than women: She cannot define and articulate her feelings.

As a result, whenever she feels something on the negative spectrum she cannot make sense of it. She tries to solve it for herself and gets increasingly irritated until it goes "boom" and she explodes.

If this story somehow seems familiar, you may find this exercise helpful. Actually, even I found the exercise useful. I can distinguish between the base categories: Anger, sadness, etc., however, these can be broken down into much more granular categories.

The more you know and can articulate your feelings in more detail, the better you will feel about yourself. This is because of a concept called emotional granularity. Developed by the psychologist, Lisa Feldman Barrett, it describes the ability to identify our emotions in specific and precise ways. By being able to pinpoint our emotions, an appropriate response can be prescribed.

It is similar to going to a doctor, but only being able to describe our pain vaguely. Is it a stinging pain or a burning pain? Where is the pain located? When did it start, and has it gotten worse? The doctor cannot provide an accurate diagnosis or treatment without these answers. It is the same with our emotions. Simply saying that we feel "bad" is vague compared to saying that we are apathetic or overwhelmed.

What is the treatment? It depends on the emotion. Rather than trying to push it away, you can ask yourself: "What is this emotion trying to tell me?" It is data. Our mind, body, and heart provide us with signals all the time, but are we paying attention to them?

When we are hungry, it is our body's way of telling us to

go eat. When we are thirsty, it tells us to go drink water. When we're feeling a challenging emotion like jealousy, it's worth examining why the emotion is coming up. What are the conditions giving rise to this emotion, and do they point to something deeper that still needs to be resolved? Through developing your emotional vocabulary, you gain power over your emotions, rather than letting them have power over you.

EXERCISE: Look regularly at the Feelings Wheel or Mood Meter and determine your current mood. Specifically, you may look at it when you have negative emotion

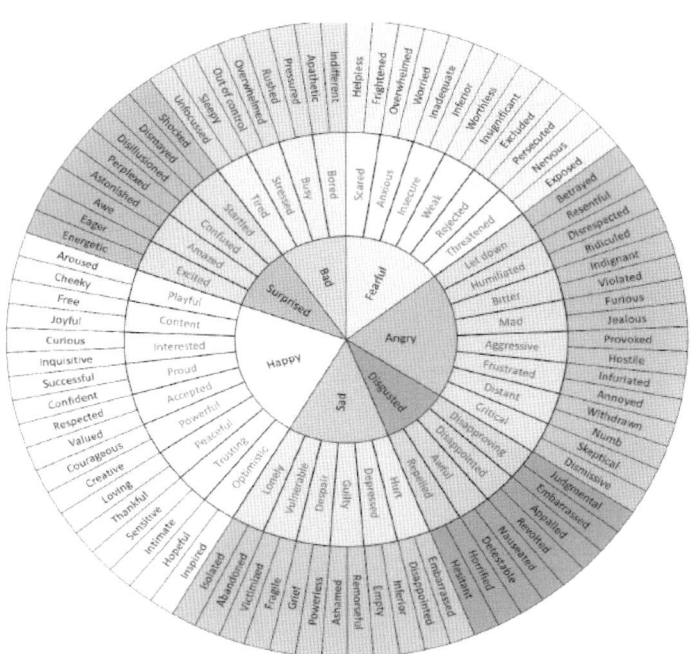

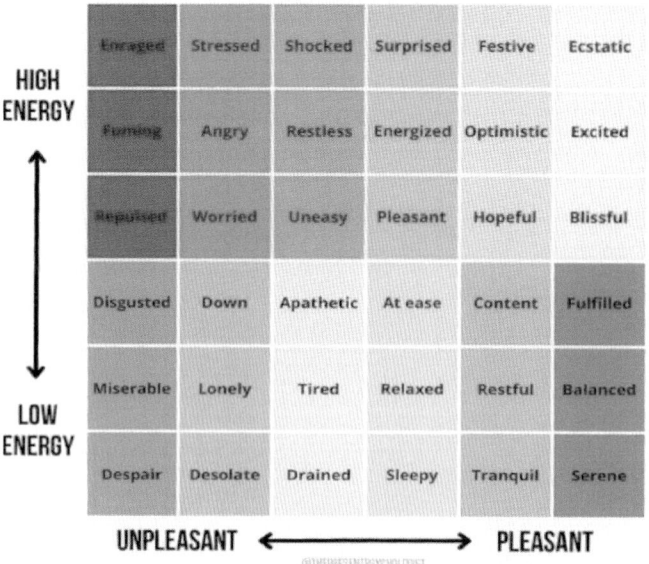

THE MOOD METER

Enraged	Stressed	Shocked	Surprised	Festive	Ecstatic
Fuming	Angry	Restless	Energized	Optimistic	Excited
Repulsed	Worried	Uneasy	Pleasant	Hopeful	Blissful
Disgusted	Down	Apathetic	At ease	Content	Fulfilled
Miserable	Lonely	Tired	Relaxed	Restful	Balanced
Despair	Desolate	Drained	Sleepy	Tranquil	Serene

HIGH ENERGY ↑ ↓ LOW ENERGY

UNPLEASANT ←——→ PLEASANT

Figure 4 The Mood Meter (Source: The Present Psychologist)

4.9 Why You Should Not Put Good/Bad Labels on What Happens

Now, we just explored how you can feel better by pointing the finger at what you feel. What if I told you that feeling bad can be avoided? Our interpretation of the things happening around us makes us feel bad. Constantly, things are happening around us, and we try to immediately make sense of them by dividing them into good and bad. Do we know if these things will turn out well or not well for us? No!

My career goal for many years was to get into one of the world's top three strategy consulting firms. I was very focused and driven. I applied and leveraged my contacts but did not achieve that goal. The application processes, and especially every rejection really got to me. I took every rejection as a "bad thing" happening to me. I am so grateful that everything happened the way it did. If I had worked in consulting, I would have been a slave with a decent salary and a big name on my business card. I am sure I would have learned something, but I would probably not have been incredibly happy. There have been so many amazing opportunities I got offered and have taken since then. I became a moderator, keynote speaker, and board member and founded my own business. I most likely would not have met Richard, and this book would still be just in our minds.

You do not know if things that happen to you are good or bad. So, stop putting labels on them. If you constantly immediately judge if what happens around you is good or bad, you create a lot of pain, stress, and drama for yourself. If things are bad or good for you, you do not know.

EXERCISE: Think about three occasions where you thought something bad happened to you that turned to be good for you.

EXERCISE: If things happen to you that you would usually judge to be bad, just accept them without putting a label on them.

4.10 Why You are Not Hurt by What Happens but by the Past

If you deal with people, you get hurt. The closer the person or the topic to you, the more it hurts, you think? Well, that is just partially right. It would be right if you would not take a package with all the past hurt with you.

Let's take criticism as an example, your partner is telling you something that you interpret as you not being good enough. The reason for this? You are thinking that about yourself. In this situation, all the situations, thoughts, and hurt from past situations that made you feel like that come up as well.

Therefore, you interpreted it worse than your partner meant it (or likely they did not mean anything in this direction) and reacted stronger than necessary. It does not help you to feel bad about it. The reason for it is that when you feel hurt by a situation or person, it is just 20% due to the current situation and 80% due to the past (Gray, 2015).

EXERCISE: Think of a time when someone hurt you. Are there any connections to past circumstances or people where you experienced something similar?

If you find yourself hurt in a situation or by a person, remember; it is just 20% due to the situation and 80% due to your past. You can decrease this 80% by practicing self-acceptance and self-care and forgiving others, which comes later.

4.11 Assess Your Social Circle

Now, most likely, you are not a loner. We all need and seek social connections. Therefore, part of your outer world is other people. As previously mentioned, the quality of your relationships determines the quality of your life. We will be assessing the quality now as a preparation for the next stage in book 2.

Let's be frank; this will hurt in the moment. The moment people are no longer good for you, or you realize that they are not real friends, it hurts. But cleaning up your social circle is like taking care of a forest: from time to time, you have to go through and remove dead or infected woods and trees, so the forest stays healthy. To replace the dead trees, and that is the beautiful part, you can plant little new trees.

If you do not do your regular walk through the forest, there will be no space for the little new trees. It is the same for your social relationships. Every one of us has 24 hours a day (minus sleep), and you have limited time available to nurture relationships, therefore you need to focus. Below is an exercise you can do to help keep your social "forest" healthy.

EXERCISE: Create four columns. The first column is for people that you are happy to have. The third column is for people who are not good for you, make you feel bad about yourself, and pull you down. Even if it is hard, being honest with yourself here is important. Even if people end up in the not good for you column, it does not mean that you must banish them from your life. It also does not necessarily mean that they are bad people. But you might want to decrease the frequency in which you see each other. The second column is for people that you are not sure which of the two other directions they fit in yet. Now that you set up your table, let me tell you how to decide best. Think about a person and follow your first instinct. Do not think too much; do it quickly: Your first instinct and gut feelings are usually right. Just write down the names of your friends and where they fall in each column. Now, in the fourth column, write who is around that could be your little trees. You could grow the relationship into a friendship.

Trust your gut feeling. It is your most helpful and accurate tool. I am a kind person and try to be tolerant. In the past, when I met a person that didn't give me the best feeling, I told myself not to be judgmental or intolerant. However, in nearly all instances, I was right. I, therefore, advise you to listen to your gut feeling. You train your gut feeling by listening to it. Your alarm system tries to stop bad people from hijacking your emotional house and your life.

I have learned one important thing in life: It does not matter how successful or beautiful someone is, when the person is ugly on the inside, it is not worth it. This person will just create pain and drama.

EXERCISE: Think of three people you had a bad feeling about at the beginning which turned out to be right.

EXERCISE: If you are meeting a person and have a bad gut feeling about them, do not ignore that feeling; stay away if you can, or be cautious and try to figure out the problem.

Another lesson I had to learn is that not having a bad gut feeling does not guarantee that a person is good or good for you. Take your time to get to know someone. One type of person your gut feeling might not identify: People who lie to themselves.

4.12 Setting and Executing Boundaries

Do you have a friend in very bad company, friends who do them no good, colleagues treating them badly or have a horrible partner? What do these people and you typi-cally have in common? They accept to be treated badly. Do you accept people not treating you the way you want? The reason for that is, again, you ACCEPT it! One important guidance in my life is: "You get what you accept!"

This saying also applies to setting boundaries. A lot of times when we are treated the way we do not want, we get mad. If we are really honest with ourselves, we are angry at the other person for overstepping our boundaries. However, we are typically even more angry and disappointed with OURSELF for ALLOWING the person to overstep our boundaries. The good thing is that once we understand that, we are no longer victims: We realize that we play an active role in the situation.

Why is it that we allow our boundaries to be overstepped? Attachment theory has some insight to provide. This scientific theory is based on the assertion that the need to be in a close relationship is embedded in our genes. John Bowlby proposed that having these close attachments allowed us a survival advantage compared to those who only relied on themselves. Although we all have a basic need to form close bonds, the way that we create them varies.

The book Attached by Amir Levine and Rachel Heller explains that in a harsh environment, a person would adapt and be intensely persistent and hypervigilant about staying close to their attachment figure. This is called an anxious attachment style.

A person with an anxious attachment style feels insecure about their relationships, and they tend to be very sensitive to small fluctuations in the behaviors of others. They can jump to conclusions about their partner (romantic or non-romantic) and try to re-establish closeness. There's a large fear of abandonment, which influences people with an anxious attachment style to stay in relationships, even if they're unhappy or their boundaries are overstepped.

Common thoughts and feelings include:
Remembering only their good qualities. Believing that even though you're unhappy, you'd better not let go, as in:
> "They can change."
> "All relationships have problems – we're not spe cial in that regard."
> "It'll take years to meet someone new; I'll end up alone."

EXERCISE: Think about three situations in the recent past where you allowed your boundaries to be over-stepped. Are some boundaries overstepped regularly? Or are there certain people that overstep your boundaries frequently? Note it down.

Here is some guidance on how to execute boundaries. In case you allow people to overstep your boundaries, there are four key strategies you can use:

1. Avoid/prevent the situation from happening: One way to avoid situations where your boundaries are over-stepped is by identifying and analyzing when or how those situations are showing up and preventing getting into such situations. You can also articulate to a person who regularly oversteps a boundary beforehand or directly before they do and let them know. Here is an example from my family. My mum is very loveable. She is more scared and often articulates her worry in a far more unpleasant way. When I told my parents that I wanted to study in the UK, their reaction was: "You cannot do that! Your English is not good enough! You will fail." She did not mean to say that she did not believe in me. As a Swiss German, my first foreign language was French, and she was worried. However, I felt like she did not have faith in me. Nowadays, it is not the master's degree but my start-up that she is concerned about. I now tell her that I do not want to talk to her about the start-up because I get discouraged by her worry, but I am happy to talk with her about everything else. If we even broach the topic, I will ask her to let us talk about something else. If that does not work, and she starts with destructive feedback, I will ask her to kindly stop, tell her that I love her and that it is better to continue our conversation another time. This boundary setting has trained my mom to learn where my boundaries are and led to a more relaxed relationship between the two of us.

EXERCISE: Think about the three occasions you noted previously. Is there a way for you to avoid these situations? Are there other occasions that you can avoid? Think about how you can avoid them. Follow my example from above and create backup scenarios of how you can prevent overstepping.

2. Remove pressure by delaying decisions: Often, our boundaries are overstepped because someone wants us to commit to something and puts us under artificial pressure to make us commit. You feel, you must make a decision at that very moment. To release the pressure, you say yes. However, as soon as you think about it, you do not feel comfortable. Or another scenario is that you agreed to do something under certain circumstances. The other person is not doing their part but still expects you to do yours.

Here is an example from my start-up. Every week, I speak with people/organizations that want to collaborate with my start-up. I listen to them and identify how I can support them. I tell them, "I can introduce you to XYZ, etc." Then, quite frequently, when it is about how they can support me, they do not commit. At the beginning, that created an internal conflict for me. I felt that I kind of committed to supporting them and introduced them to people; however,

I did that under the assumption that the other party was willing to support me too. (I am happy to support other people without getting anything in return, but partnerships/collaborations should be two-sided.) When that was not the case, I felt it was hard to step back from my offer but felt used if I did the intros. I had to learn to go out of the meeting and say, "Let me think about our potential partnership. I will get back to you." By doing that, I also learned that it is okay to change my mind because, for example, I receive new information. Learn that you do not have to react at the moment and that it is okay to change your mind!

EXERCISE: Do not allow others to put you under time pressure when demanding a decision from you. Train delaying a response, if people ask you for favors. Practice with people you know will not take it wrong. E.g., "Can you help me with XX?" and you respond, "Let me think about it, I will get back to you!" or, if you can, say no directly. Try not to put yourself under pressure by promising when you will respond. You can practice that in a low-risk environment. You need to practice so that you are able to say it when you are under pressure.

3. Remember, it is your primary job to take care of yourself: If you find it very hard executing boundaries, it might be that you have conflicting beliefs. E.g., by helping a friend you have to choose between letting your friend down and letting yourself down because you are overworked and need rest. Because you do not want to hurt another person's feelings, you then might end up hurting your own feelings. You often might not feel good about having said yes, but did you realize that you preferred hurting yourself over others? That is not taking care of yourself! REMIND yourself here, that you are not hurting that person's feelings but your own. It is your number one job to take care of yourself. Find an ideal solution where no one gets hurt.

EXERCISE: If you are asked for a favor and know it hurts you, remind yourself: It is your number one job to take care of yourself!

4. Identify the beliefs that cause you to allow people to overstep your boundaries: Another reason for struggling to execute boundaries is that it might be tied to your values and beliefs. I am generous and like to give gifts and invite people for a coffee or a meal. When I started my start-up, I wanted to continue being generous, like when I had a great manager salary. It was very hard for me to recognize and implement that as a founder, I need to invite other people less but rather request to split the bill. On these occasions, it often did not even need the other person to overstep the boundaries because of conflicts with the belief that "I am generous." I did that myself. This belief generally is not bad, unless you implement it in a way that hurts you and makes you overstep your boundaries. In my case, I did. I should not have invited people out all the time because I am a founder bootstrapping my own start-up, and it is my responsibility to take care of myself and my baby (my start-up) first.

EXERCISE: Give the rational part of your brain a name and the creative part. Tell your rational side that you know it is trying to be good. Then, ask why? If the response comes to mind, say thank you. Now move to the creative past – ask that part how you can solve that challenge. Write down at least five ideas presented to you. Suggest these ideas to the first part of your brain and ask if it would be open to trying them out. Let that part of your brain know that if it does not work, it can go to its default mode. Say thank you.

4.13 Forgiving Yourself and Others

One important thing is to be at peace with yourself and others in order to be happy. We just covered when people overstep your boundaries—when you ALLOW people to overstep your boundaries. If that happens, you become a bit mad at the other person and probably quite disappointed in yourself for allowing that breach. Here are two exercises that help you to forgive yourself and others.

EXERCISE: To forgive yourself. Go in front of a mirror and tell yourself that you are very sorry and did not intend to hurt yourself.

EXERCISE: To forgive someone else, tell them you were hurt as soon as possible. The longer you allow a grudge and the hurt to stay with you without doing anything, the more it affects you. It is like venom. You can approach the person in real life and tell them how it made you feel. Tell the person that you forgive him/ her. Feel the forgiveness. Feel the weight lifting from your shoulders. If you do not want to do it in real life, you can imagine looking the person in the eyes and telling it to them. Don't forget, it is about you forgiving, not about their reaction.

If you hold on to anger and grudge, you punish yourself most. It keeps you stuck in a dark place, and you cannot walk into a bright future if you cannot let go. I saw people that ruin their whole life with it. It is not worth it.

4.14 The Love Letter Exercise

The love letter exercise was developed by John Gray and further explored in Men are from Mars, Women are from Venus as a tool to improve your relationship with yourself and in romantic relationships. I found it to be really helpful for forgiving oneself and others. The short version of the exercise is that you write yourself or the other person you want to forgive a letter (you can, but do not have to share it with that person — it is primary for yourself). Let's get directly to the exercise:

EXERCISE: Dear XX, I am writing this letter to share my feelings. And then you share 1–2 sentences where you express something related to the respective feeling:

Anger: E.g., I do not like... I feel frustrated...
Sadness: I feel disappointed... It makes me sad...
Fear: I am afraid... I worry...
Regret: I am sorry... I did not want...
Love: I appreciate... I thank...

4.15 Increasing Empathy

If people annoy you, remind yourself that, in most cases, people all wake up and want to be accepted, loved, and do well. They do not wake up to upset you. Everyone is doing their best every day. What helps is to increase your em-pa-thy for others. The exercise below will help you with it by expanding the love and empathy you have for people (e.g., your pets) who deeply care about others. By doing the exercise regularly, I recommend daily, you increase your empathy! A nice side effect, you will also feel better about yourself, and it will be much easier for you to connect with people. Being empathic towards people helps you to see the good in them!

EXERCISE: Close your eyes and think about a person or animal you care a lot about. Feel this feeling deeply. Give it a color. Extend that color to your room, the building, all the people there, your area, your city, country, and the world. Say I love you and mean it in the end.

Chapter 5 – Self-Development

5.1 Comfort Zone vs. Growth Zone*

For some, it is the sofa and watching Netflix or TV. For others, it is always seeing the same people, working in the same role, going to the same restaurant, or travelling to the same holiday destination. The comfort zone has different faces. But one thing is for sure, even if it feels comfy and safe in the short term, if you enjoy it for too long, it keeps you stuck and makes you unhappy. The good thing is that you have the key to get unstuck, and we are helping you to get out of there asap! Ready!?

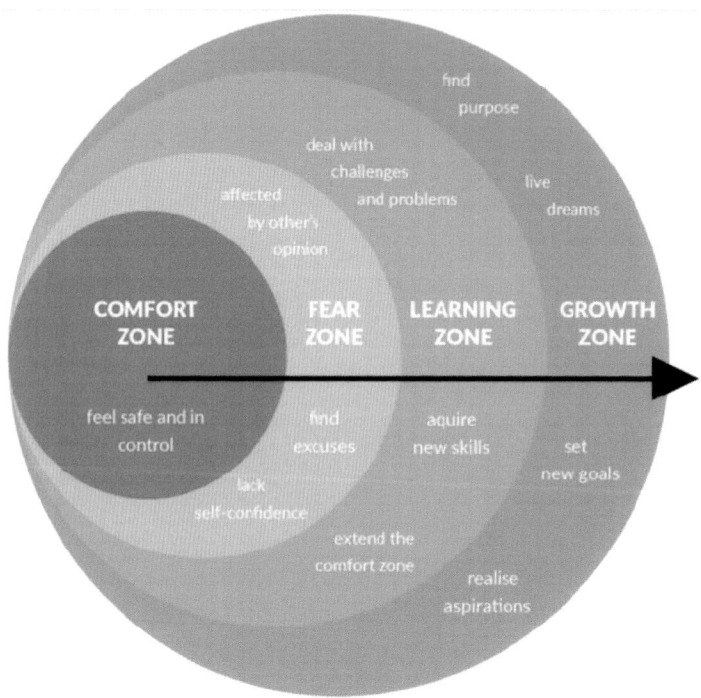

Figure 5 Comfort Zone to Growth Zone (Source: Positive Psychology)

Figure 5 was developed by Hugo Alberts and Lucinda Poole as a visual aid for people to understand the costs of staying in the comfort zone and the necessity to leave this zone for the experience of growth.

If you think about a baby taking their first steps, they will stumble and fall many times before they get the hang of it. At some point in our lives, we do everything for the first time, and accept that challenges and failures will be associated with it. Learning to ride a bike involves falling and getting back up. Eventually, you learn how to ride the bike fluently, and you've grown. This is the same when it comes to connecting with others.

The comfort zone is where we feel safe and in control. There is low risk of failure or rejection or any other unpleasant experiences. However, there's little to no room for growth because we just do what we know, over and over. Grant Cordone says, "Comfort makes more prisoners than all the jails combined!"

Anxiety is telling you there is a perceived threat; it is our mind's way of trying to protect us. You get a dopamine hit every time you avoid a situation that would cause you anxiety, but over time, it can lead to isolation. Like learning to ride a bicycle, it requires us to leave our comfort zone and step into the fear zone. This can be very uncomfortable, because it's chock-full of uncertainty, and we often make excuses to try to avoid this space.

However, if you are able to muster up the courage to endure the zone, you will come out on the other side and into the learning zone. This is where you can acquire new skills and learn to deal with challenges. Once you make it to the learning zone, you actually extend your comfort zone, meaning that you begin to feel comfortable in what was previously uncomfortable.

When you stay long enough in the learning zone, you start to redefine yourself in terms of what you can do, and you have grown as a person on multiple levels. You may experience a sense of meaning by investing time into something that really matters to you and creating a pathway that makes it easier for you to follow your dreams. You have gained on a more fundamental, personal level. Entering the growth zone is the ultimate reward for enduring the fear zone.

Embracing fear can eventually become a habit and overall lifestyle. The catchphrase for the YouTube channel Yes Theory is: "Seek discomfort." Rather than avoiding it, you are intentionally leaning into it because you realize that learning and growing go hand-in-hand with stepping outside your comfort zone. You might be thinking to yourself: "But how do I face my fears?"Exercise: Here is a step-by-step process that you can utilize to get from your comfort zone to your growth zone:

Step 1 – Comfort Zone
Thinking about your social skills and connections, is there something on the horizon that will require you to step outside your comfort zone and into the fear zone? Or is there something you would like to do but fear holding you back from doing it?

Examples include declining an invitation to an event where you do not know many people, opting not to join a club, or not reaching out to a friend to see if you can hang out. Another example, having all the things required to start your own business but fearing leaping. Describe this situation.

Step 2 – Fear Zone
What would you experience if you were to step outside your comfort zone into the fear zone? In other words, what characterizes your fear? For instance, would you feel anxious, notice your heart beating faster, sense a lack of self-confidence, or have critical thoughts such as, "I can't do this" or "I'm not smart enough for this"?
List as many fear signs that you can think of.

Step 3 – Learning Zone
What opportunities for learning would you miss by staying within your comfort zone?
For instance, by declining an invitation to an event where you don't know many people, you are missing out on building your social skills, potentially making new friends, and having a good time. List the most important learning opportunities you miss by staying in your comfort zone.

Step 4 – Growth Zone
Consider your potential for growth if you were to stay in the learning zone for quite some time. How might this transform you as a person? What could you gain at a more fundamental, personal level by this learning? How could your growth affect your relationships with others?

This can also be visualized within a table:

	Staying in comfort zone	Stepping outside of comfort zone
What's the benefit?	Being in a predictable, safe environment	Growing as a person, developing resiliency, improving skills, connecting with new people, creating a sense of achievement, etc.
What's the cost?	Missing opportunities for learning, not living to your full potential, feeling isolated, feeling stuck, etc.	Being uncomfortable

Table 1 Comfortability Matrix

As you look at the benefits and costs, it might become evident to you how much it's costing you physically, emotionally, and mentally to stay within your comfort zone. If you're able to bare the feeling of being uncomfortable, there is so much you can gain.

What may also help is reframe your mindset when it comes to failure. F.A.I.L. as an acronym that stands for: First Attempt In Learning. In this way, failure doesn't evoke shame. Failure is part of the process of learning. A similar term I've heard is to have a "prototype mindset." In the realm of design thinking, prototyping refers to creating a scaled-down version of the product in order to reveal any problems with the current design. In other words, they are expecting to see it fail. It allows them to fail quickly and cheaply, and utilize the data from those failures to refine their process and end product.

This may all sound very scientific, but approaching it from this lens might empower you to take action, because your feelings of inadequacy and shame aren't as suffocating. Data is data. Data is neutral information, and sometimes we apply an extra unnecessary layer of interpretation on top of it. I learned this when I was studying music at university. For example, when a musician plays a "wrong" note, it simply means what they inputted did not match their intended output. This is the raw data. However, it's easy for musicians to be hard on themselves. They apply an extra layer of interpretation: "I played a wrong note and, therefore, I am a bad musician." Not only does this burden the person with shame, but it also creates additional frustration, disappointment, and discouragement.

In other words, it's not neutral.
When it comes to connecting with others, you may have

thoughts like: "I sounded awkward in this conversation, and, therefore, I am bad at connecting with people."

Richard`s flute teacher wrote a blog post once that made him understand the importance of having a neutral mindset when it comes to learning. Learning from a neutral mindset allows you to connect with people in a more grounded, enjoyable way. It doesn't cause your sense of self-worth to fluctuate wildly. You are simply observing data, and adjusting your input if it doesn't match your intended output. Your self-worth doesn't need to be tied to the outcome or how well you performed.

"I am still learning." – Francisco de Goya. This quote is inscribed on the University of Lethbridge's wall and is a good reminder about lifelong learning. It is about an intrinsic motivation to learn and grow, rather than frantically trying to prove yourself to receive external validation.

5.2 Happiness in the Now vs. Having a Vision for the Future

So when happiness is not being in the comfort zone, what is it then? Let me introduce you to a very helpful framework.

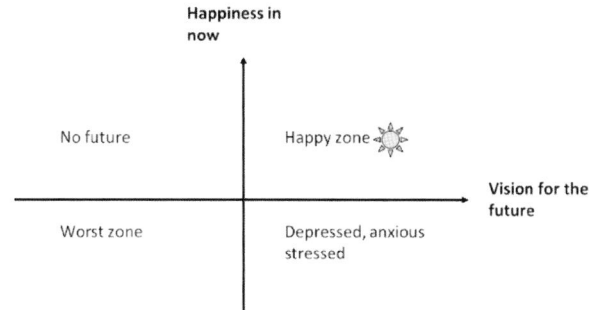

Figure 3 Happiness Matrix (Vishen Lakhiani)

EXERCISE: Let's do an exercise together. Above there is a matrix, on one axis, it says, "Happiness in the now," and on the other one, it says, "Vision for the future." Happiness in the now means, how happy are you in the moment? Vision for the future means, do you know where you are going? Make a dot where you think you are. Please repeat that exercise after reading the book and see how the result changed (Happiness Matrix by The Code of the Extraordinary Mind, Vishen Lakhiani, borrowed).

If you are like most people, you end up in the lower right corner. You have a vision for the future, but you are not really happy in the now. You feel anxious, stressed, and depressed. Why is that the case? I can tell you. While both dimensions are important, you are doing one thing wrong and tying one dimension to the other. What do I mean? You likely tie the happiness in the now to how well you progress toward your vision.

EXERCISE: Remember the last time you were working towards something for a significant amount of time. You really put in the effort; you achieved it finally. Be honest, how long did the resulting excitement and happiness last?

We are always working towards goals. We believe if we achieve a goal and then we will be happy. However, this happiness does not last long, and we replace the goal we achieved with another one, and the cycle starts again. Do you understand why the happiness in the now is not working for you?

I've been reflecting a lot over the past few months on what truly brings happiness to my life. Happiness felt like a fleeting thing that I was always trying to pursue. Through my upbringing and societal messaging, I was instilled with the general sense that happiness is something that can be obtained, that it's an end state or destination. In other words, once I earn a degree, secure a well-paying job, buy a house, and raise a family, then I'll live happily ever after. The issue is that we get stuck on a hedonic treadmill.

Coined by Philip Brickman and Donald Campbell, the concept of a hedonic treadmill refers to how humans quickly return to a relatively stable level of happiness despite major positive or negative events or life changes. Remind yourself of a time that you made a purchase that you thought would bring you happiness. How long did that feeling last, and how do you feel about it right now? Chances are that the initial peak of euphoria quickly subsided, and you returned back to a baseline level of happiness. And so, we keep buying new gadgets, striving for accolades, looking for a bigger paycheck, and indulging in entertainment and other pleasurable activities, to keep getting hits of happiness. It's as though we have a hole in our hearts, and we're continuously searching for the block that will fit and finally make us feel whole. We're still running on the treadmill.

Talking about your vision. You need to have a vision that excites you so much that it makes you jump out of your bed in the morning. Ideally, it is something that not just you but also other people or the world benefit from! We are going into goal-setting a bit later!

You can solve it by having the vision for the future and enjoying the now, independently of your progress toward your vision. Untie both dimensions, and you are out of the trap!

Generally, happiness has two components. You need a future vision that appeals to you, and you need to be happy in the now and appreciate the moment (your baseline happiness at that moment). The most important thing is that you need to have both and see these independently of each other!

So for me, the vision is: If I am not here one day, I want to have touched the people I met positively. That I made them feel respected, loved, believed in, supported, and empowered. I hope that they did not feel alone, that I helped them to believe in themselves, that I gave them power to make their visions come true, and that others and the world benefit from that.

EXERCISE: The main lesson here: Check out (regularly)—do you have a compelling vision? If not, we help you in later chapters with that. Are you happy in the now? If not, check with yourself, is it because you are making your happiness dependent on your progress toward your goals?

5.3 Happiness in the Now: How the Reverse Gap Pushes Your Sense of Achievement

We just talked about happiness in the now and how we sometimes have a gap between where we are and the goal we want to achieve. Instead of looking at the future and what you lack to get to where you want to be, you may want to look backward and recognize what you have achieved! You might want to look at your reverse gap instead: Select a point in the past and look at what you have achieved since then! The related exercise will use gap thinking towards your benefit and increase your sense of achievement, remind you of your capabilities, and will increase your happiness in the now.

EXERCISE: This exercise is called "Reverse Gap": Write down what you achieved in the last year, last five years, or define another time period. What have you achieved since then, write it down. Take a moment to acknowledge your achievements. Celebrate yourself.

Revisit your responses when you are scared of failing or scared of the future, or you are on a self-confidence low. What also helps is if you read your past journal entries from the past. You will remember what you struggled with and how much you have achieved and overcome since then!

5.4 A Balanced Life is a Happy Life

Remember that we talked about baseline happiness earlier? To have a good baseline happiness, it is important that you live a balanced life. You can divide your life into different areas such as love life, friendships, financial stability, etc. With a balanced life, I mean that you are doing at least okay in all of these areas in your life. For example, imagine you are at school, and you are getting good to very good grades everywhere, and let's say you have three subjects that you failed. You will not be able to enjoy all your good grades, because you will be worried about repeating the year. It is similar in life.

When working in Singapore for a large consulting firm, I quickly met new people and was soon invited to all kinds of nice gatherings. As a European, I really enjoyed this kind of tropical expat life. I moved to a beautiful and fancy condo. It had an Olympic-size pool, jacuzzi, a putting green, terraces, a gym, and a clubhouse. I was working hard and de-stressed by running along the coast, swimming, and then going into the jacuzzi every day. I worked crazy hours.

To remain sociable, I took my lunch break, took one or two after-work drinks with people, got home, did my workout, and then continued working. Sometimes, during the week or at the weekend, I was invited to some party, which meant even less sleep. I managed to get promoted as one of the few expats there after only one year, and also had a good social life. However, the continuous sleep deprivation made me feel more moody and unsatisfied. It was fun, but I knew this was not sustainable. The sleep deprivation would start taking its toll on my health and, eventually, my work performance. As I wanted to enjoy the little spare time with fun things and Singapore is not cheap, I did not really save money and knew that if I lost my job (it is not that difficult in Singapore), I would be screwed. While your notice period after probation is around one month, your rental contracts are normally two years. Your visa and health insurance are tied to your employment. If you lose your employment, you lose both. Even if you are employed, if you get too sick, your health insurance might not cover or at least not everything (they have limits).

Why am I telling you this? While I was doing great in many areas of my life, I had an amazing time, my lifestyle was not sustainable. I wasn't taking enough care of my health and or my financial security as required in a country like Singapore. I was lucky, and I guess I left at the right time, but this also could have really gone wrong, and I knew it deep in my heart.

If you want to be happy, you need a balanced life, which means you do fairly well in every area of your life. It is something I had to learn the hard way. If you do exceptionally great in some areas of your life, and poor in others, your life is unbalanced, and you will not be happy.

I developed 13 categories I believe we need for a fulfilled and balanced life. Feel free to customize the categorization for yourself:

1. Love relationships
2. Friendships
3. Family Life
4. Your Home
5. Physical Wellbeing
6. Mental Wellbeing
7. Financial Situation
8. Career / Working Life
9. Continuous Learning
10. Creative Life
11. Adventures
12. Spiritual/religious Life
13. Community Service

EXERCISE: For the 13 areas, rank yourself from 1–10. 1 being poor and 10 being super!

EXERCISE: Now that you have the results, look at which areas you rank the lowest in. Why? You may focus on improving the lowest ones. Think about what to learn and do to improve.

I advise you to focus on at least being okay in all areas of your life, not just for now but also in the future. I advise you to set goals for every category. Do have mitigation mechanisms to prevent slipping. If you want to have financial freedom, get yourself an emergency fund. Want to stay healthy, do regular checkups, etc. I recommend you to think about preventing slipping instead of firefighting. I established an early warning system for the different categories. For example, health-wise, if I get above a certain weight (I won't tell you what that is), that is my trigger to cut sugar and workout more often. Regarding my continuous learning, my lowest boundary, I read at least one book a week. Now, these minimum thresholds are not goals, this is the minimum effort or your thres-hold that you commit to; if you go below it, you really take action!

EXERCISE: Establish early warnings for every category. These should be measurable indicators easy for you to track/tell. Define the thresholds and countermeasures in case you breach your thresholds.

5.5 Gap and Gain in Goal Setting*

When setting your vision, evaluating if you are in a "Gap" or "Gain" mindset is important. This is a concept developed by Dan Sullivan, the Founder of Strategic Coach. In short, people end up feeling disappointed when they measure the gap between what they achieved and their ideal. They feel like they've fallen short and failed.

By contrast, being in a „Gain" mindset is measuring yourself against your past self and recognizing the progress you've made. This inspires a feeling of success, satisfaction, and further motivation. Here are some examples to illustrate this concept: Say I have set a goal to run for 30 minutes each day for a week. I end up running 4 out of 7 days. I am in a „Gap" mindset if I say, „I failed because I missed three days." I am in a „Gain" mindset if I say things like, „I still ran four days, and I noticed how energized, and healthy I felt after doing those runs."

Did you know that out of the Olympic athletes that are placed on the podium, the silver medalists are the most unhappy? The gold medalists are happy because they got 1st, and the bronze medalists are happy because they barely squeaked into the podium. The silver medalist is unhappy because they're thinking, „I didn't get gold. I fell short because I only got second." They measure against their ideal, and thus they're in the „Gap." They aren't recognizing that they're literally the top second athlete in the world in that sport (a „Gain" mindset ; Goldman, 2012).

Being in the Gain mindset means that both of the following statements are true:

1. Having an intense commitment to succeed; and
2. Having a healthy detachment from what you're doing.

You can have a vision of the future but also not need it in order to feel happy. You already have everything you need in the here and now. Psychologists have separated need and want into two core types of passion: obsessive and harmonious.

An obsessive passion is highly impulsive and fueled by suppressed emotions and unresolved internal conflict. You become obsessed with something to the point of an unhealthy desperation. You believe you need it, and can't be happy without it. By contrast, harmonious passion is intrinsically motivated and healthy. You control your passion rather than have it control you. You're purposeful and goal-directed, not "need"-driven.

This may sound counterintuitive, but the reality is that by no longer needing what you want, you are actually far more enabled to get it. Dan Sullivan says: "I don't think we set and achieve goals in an effort to become happy. We do it because we are happy and want to expand our happiness."

5.6 Goal Setting Basics

There are so many different approaches to goal setting. I found the goal setting method "Your three most important questions" in The Code of the Extraordinary Mind by Vishen Lakhiani helpful. I am applying it to myself. There are three types of goals important for humankind: The

experiences you want to make, where you want to grow, and how you want to contribute. We've all heard the saying, "Buy experiences, not things." You likely had your own experience that a fun trip with great friends was much more rewarding than buying a fancy new bag or TV. The second area: Growth. I believe everything in life grows or dies; the same goes for people. Statistics show that people who retire earlier also die earlier than those who retire later! Many people desperately wait to retire without a plan and then die because they do not learn anymore, do not grow anymore, and lack purpose. Let's get to the third category: Contributing to the world or other people's lives. This point is so important. People who are not just focused on themselves but about how to contribute are much happier. Why do you think so many wealthy people engage in philanthropy: It is a win–win.
Let's do the exercise:

EXERCISE: Take a piece of paper in landscape format and use a pen to divide the paper into three columns. The headings are: 1. Experiences, 2. Growth and 3. Contribution. Write down in bullets in column 1, the experiences you want to have, in column 2, where you want to grow, and in column 3, in which way you want to contribute to other people's life and the world. Best to do it with a pencil so you can change bits after reading the next chapters.

5.7 Why you Should Have Non–money Related Goals

Now, you never know how life will turn out. You might have times when money is tight or you do not have money at all. Especially for times like that, when you might feel everything is falling apart and you are under immense pressure, it is especially important to have goals that you can actually achieve. Therefore, review your sheet and check for how many of the goals you have written down you need money to achieve them. Not all your goals should be tied to money. You should be able to achieve at least some of your goals without it.

I wrote for experiences that I want to: Enjoy a walk in nature every day and feel the wind blowing through my hair. For growth: Learn how to listen better when others speak and be more empathetic towards others. For contribution: I want to make at least three people smile per day and make the people I meet feel appreciated and loved.

EXERCISE: In each of the three columns (experiences you want to have, areas you want to grow, areas you want to contribute), add at least two bullet points with things you do not need money for.

5.8 About Moonshots and Baby Steps

One mistake I believe most of us make is thinking too small. To summarize it, most think very small. Why is that a mistake? Because our minds are programmed to achieve the goals we set: ACHIEVE, not overachieve!

When you go into a salary negotiation with your boss and aim for a pay raise of 5%, if you are negotiating well, you will go out there with 5%, and you will fully achieved your goal! Are you proud of yourself now? Hold your horses! Inflation is rising, you really did a good job, you might have asked for 10%. Even if you walked out of your boss's office and did not achieve your full goal, you got, let's say, 7%, more than with your first strategy, just by asking for more. Ask yourself for more, ask life for more, and ask your brain for more!

The lesson here: set bigger goals! Even if you fail at some or do not achieve them fully, you get much, much further than someone who sets small goals. And you know, achieving goals or networking works like compound interest. They do not develop linearly but are cumulative!

So let's apply the above example to moonshots. Moonshots are super ambitious goals that are unrealistic and difficult to achieve. An ambitious goal for my start-up would be to get X customers and Y revenues per year.

A moonshot goal would be to make my start-up the most valuable social network in the world. You get the difference? By the way, big innovative entrepreneurs and companies such as Richard Branson or Google think that way. They have a vivid vision in their mind that makes them jump out of bed and propels them. They think, let's build a rocket that can fly to Z, they do not think, I have this amazing Excel Sheet with 6357 To Dos. Even if some of your projects fail or you do not fully achieve all goals you have, believe me, you will get much, much further than if you set realistic goals. Hey, failing in some projects is not that bad. Google has, for example, a lot of successful projects, but also some that did not make it. Look at, for example, The Google X company aimed to expand internet connectivity via Balloons. They closed down the project because they could not get the cost low enough. Google still exists and is seen as a front runner, despite the several failed projects because they were able to pull off some truly amazing stuff.

Now, the tricky part about moonshots is that, in most cases, there is no straight roadmap to it. That is where you have to take baby steps. A baby step is a move you make in the direction that you think is right. You make a small step after step.

Let me give you an example. You are staying at a new friend's house for the first time, and are not entirely familiar with the house's layout. In the night, you wake up, and it is raining heavily. You can hear it dripping some-where, and you guess right; the window is open, and water is coming inside. You carefully leave the bed and start walking, taking slow, small steps toward where you think the door is, battling the dark. You feel with your hands, try to find a light switch or the door. You hear the noise of the water and follow it. Maybe you get lost in between, the sound gets less loud, and you realize you are moving in the wrong direction. Your baby-step journey to your moonshot works similarly!

Many of us have a long to-do list full of very small and insignificant items we get lost in. Do you get inspired by those kind of goals? Probably not! Do you know what is on the to-do list of people who think big, like Richard Branson? Buy an airline. Now we are talking. You might think, well, Richard Branson can afford it, but I...

Even some huge and successful companies are setting such moonshot goals. Don't play safe, take a calculated risk. Go for moonshots!

EXERCISE: Ensure that at least half of your goals in every category are moonshots!

Now you have a moonshot goal and do not know how to achieve it? The answer is easy! Take baby steps, do the thing that brings you closer to your goal. Try it out and, like being in a fog, you are just doing one step after each other and continuously checking if the overall direction is right.

EXERCISE: Pick out a moonshot and try to figure out the next baby step you can take!

5.9 Finding and Applying Your Character Strength for a Bliss State

Were you ever so drawn into about a project that you literally forgot to eat? (I do not say that meal–skipping is good though.) Most likely, you were in a bliss state while working. What would you say if you could be in that state most of the time during your work? Yes, that's possible!

Nowadays, people are mostly concerned with WHAT they do for work. If they are not happy, they change companies. However, it's not what you do but how you do it! While most of us hopefully develop our own personality in our private or business life, it is often not the case. Our bosses usually train or expect us to do our work in the way and manner they do, whether it fits our personality or not. Applying our key strength in how we work enables us to play out our strength, becoming more authentic at work and, most likely, more visible and successful.

I started the first years of my career in big consulting/accounting firms. Big companies are often well structured, because they have to be so that they can function. In big organizations, you have a lot of governance, processes, and procedures. There are ways to do things. It is a very good place for learning. You usually learn how to work the way your superior works or maybe like your colleagues do. Most people adjust to it well, and it somehow works for them.

I also functioned most of the time the way I was expected. After all, I felt I had no other choice because I wanted to fit in and be accepted to move forward in the organization. However, with me having ADD (Attention Deficit Disorder), this fitting in and doing things how they were expected to be done, really bothered me: Sitting in long, inefficient meetings annoyed me; working from one place or on one topic for a long time bored me; doing activities similar to audits, PowerPoint presentations where everything had to be super, super accurate was not to my liking. It drove me nuts and I really needed my daily workouts to blow off steam.

When I was younger, I tried to hide my ADD. I was disciplined enough, and my ADD was not that strong that it would be that obvious. Today, I consider it one of my great strengths. I would probably perform average in a (for me) boring 9-5 job; however, I am above average, managing multiple projects simultaneously. I regularly have people asking me, "How do you do that? How do you sleep?" What is the difference between my career start and today? I was lucky to have a manager job in Venture Capital where I was given all the freedom you could wish for, and I started doing things my way. I applied my strengths to how I do things. I had a team of around 15 people, and I led them with empathy, love, guidance, kindness, interest, motivation, and inspiration. I focused on my strengths: Leadership, strategic and conceptual thinking, and creativity, and outsourced things where I was weak to my team. Developing concepts, presentations, or important emails would mean delivering at an 80% status, so I delegated them to team members who were more detail-oriented. They enjoyed employing their own strengths!

I advise you to identify your key strengths and apply them in the way HOW you work to achieve your goal. This will massively improve your happiness at work. There are many personality tests out there. I can definitely recommend the below test (currently free); however, you can also take another comparable test and do the exercise with it.

EXERCISE: The VIA Institute offers an assessment that tells people their 24 character strengths, and ranks them based on their top five signature strengths, middle strengths, and lesser strengths. It can be found here: https://www.viacharacter.org. Write down your five key strengths. For the next two weeks, regularly look at these strengths and find ways to use them in the way HOW you do your work. Write down your experience after two weeks. What worked, what did not? How did your happiness and performance develop? What feedback did you receive from your boss and your peers? Keep what worked for you!!!

For example, my top five strengths are:

1. Forgiveness
2. Curiosity
3. Love of Learning
4. Fairness
5. Social Intelligence

Taken together, I see the world from a people-focused lens and one where I'm endlessly curious about getting to know others better. I treat others with compassion and try my best to see things from the perspective of others, even if I may personally disagree. I forgive those that have wronged me, because at the end of the day, I see them as fellow humans. Humans are imperfect and they make mistakes, even those who have intentionally hurt me in a significant way. I try not to harbor ill will and vengeance.

By coming to understand your top strengths, you will

be able to embody your authentic self. You are connected with yourself and don't need to pretend that you are someone who you are not. I am excited to hear how that worked out for you!!

5.10 We all have 24 hours. Why should we replace entertainment with education?

In many ways, there is inequality in the world which are great excuses for not being where you want to be. However, time is a different thing. Richard Branson, Elon Musk, Joe Biden, and you, all have 24 hours per day. Sure, some people need slightly more or less sleep. However, the big question is: "What do you do with your 24 hours?" It is not that much about what you say you are or what you say that you do. What you do reveals who you are and what is important to you.

I have my start-up, am wrapping up my PhD, have a board position, am doing keynote speaking and moderation, writing this book, and much more, and yes, I sleep. I also meet up with friends and I have fun. Even though many people around me complain that they are stressed, they do not have time to meet or do things they want to do. I do not arrogantly look at this, but it makes me smile every time. Most of these people have a 9–5 type of job or are at least employed. They work their socks off for someone else's dream. They are not inspired, and it sucks the life out of them to live that life. To compensate, they rest on the sofa after work and binge-watch TV or Netflix. On the weekend, they go out partying. They live from weekend to weekend, from holiday to holiday, or they focus on family. Now, why is that? "Bread and games." According to this motto, the old Roman people are numbing their un-inspirational life with distraction. It might feel pleasant, but you live a low-energy life and are stuck in a hamster wheel. You have enough time, but not enough energy.

Spending time purely on entertainment can be fun in the short-term but can ultimately lead to wasting time on the things that truly matter in life. Instead of just chasing after fun, use that time to read, learn, grow, do sports, and develop. I know it is counter-intuitive because in our educational system, we learned early on that school/work is tough and playing is fun. But let's be honest, how do you feel after binge-watching your favorite series? Maybe you are a bit guilty that you did not do anything productive for hours. Maybe you feel sad because you have fallen from this great imaginary and exciting life you see in the series into your boring, real life? Now, even though it might feel hard to start, how do you feel after reading two chapters of a great personal development book, and you have some key insights that you feel are changing your life, or you went to an event and met a super inspiring person? When we are really honest, we feel better when we learn and grow than when we are just being entertained. I watch Netflix only. occasionally. I often get this feeling while watching and say to myself, "Why should I watch someone living an amazing life on TV or Netflix when I can use this time to create my own amazing life?"

EXERCISE: Imagine how you want your life to be. If you think about indulging in entertainment, remind yourself: Do you want to waste your time watching other people have an amazing life, or do you want to use your time, to create the life you want!?

5.11 Variation Increases Happiness – An Ice Cream Experiment

Do you have a favorite dish? What is it? Would you still like it if you needed to eat it for one week in a row every day? I love Malaga ice cream, and I think having one every day would be okay. However, I guess it would just become less special. There is a study, funnily, it is really on ice cream—that is mentioned in The Science of Well-Being, Yale University, Prof Laurie Santos; look up the exact experiment. The findings show that if you vary the ice cream, it provides you with more happiness. Which means you can increase your happiness with very little means. You can vary the way you go to work, the food you buy/order, the workouts you do, etc. This trick gives you an unlimited number of ways to improve your happiness. These are all ways to grow your curiosity and push you slightly out of your comfort zone.

EXERCISE: Where in your life do you always do the same thing? Think about how you can vary and do it!

5.12 Exploring Yourself

I believe every one of us is like a little globe. Depending on which angle and from which distance we look at a person, we will always explore something new. See yourself as a little globe. Explore tiny bits of yourself. You most likely know some skills and preferences of yours already. However, the more you explore, the more you will discover, and the better you will get to know yourself.
I feel very lucky that I have tried so many sports and hobbies. I got to love especially sailing and polo. Am I super good at it? No, but who cares. Do it as long as you enjoy it. No explanation needed! I am also very grateful for exploring myself so much in my career. I am now thirty-three, and I worked in risk management consulting, did a doctorate, worked in Venture Capital, as a moderator, as a manager, and now as a founder and author. I am very grateful because I found out that I love moderation, key-

note speaking, writing, and being a founder. While in the earlier days I was scrutinized for my CV because I apparently changed positions and fields too often, nowadays I am, like other people, celebrated for it. We have CVs of the future. Don't be scared.

EXERCISE: Note down hobbies or career paths you want to try and just start. Try new stuff to identify passions and talents and get to know yourself better.

5.13 Hard Things First

This is especially helpful for you if you struggle with procrastination. You must start your day by doing the hardest thing first. Then, everything after it will feel easier for you, and you will already have a sense of achievement early in the day. Compared if you (like you are probably doing right now) save the hard thing for later, it will be hanging over your head like a dark cloud for the whole day (and most likely even much longer).

EXERCISE: In the evening, write down what you want to do the next day. Listen to your gut, what activity you feel most resistant to and reluctant about, and circle it. Then, start with that activity first the next day.

If you find it too hard to start with the hard thing right now, you might want to start with establishing some simple routine you do directly after getting up. Because you are directly getting into action (not in overthinking), you get a little sense of achievement and reduce procrastination regarding subsequent activities.

EXERCISE: Establish a small ritual that you do directly after leaving bed. This can be making your bed as the first thing or drinking a glass of water. Do that consistently every day from the moment you wake up. Once that works well, start adding the exercise with doing the hard thing as the first big activity of the day.

5.14 Delayed Gratification

It is great if you work hard and do the hard thing first. However, finding a balance between hard work and gratification is important.

With my start-up, I am mainly working in my home office. This means I can organize myself. Same with my PhD in the past. It is too easy to get distracted. Also, with a long-term project like a PhD or start-up, you might lose motivation because you might feel that you are not progressing (fast enough) on some days. Sure, you definitely take breaks regularly. But I do not work that much time focused. I do not say, I work four hours and then stop and reward myself. I tell myself. When I complete this chapter, I am done for today and will enjoy a hot bath with candles around it. Or what is even better, I put myself under slight pressure and make plans for the evening. Then I estimate what goals I can achieve and work hard so I can finish on time. This way, I am motivated. I have ambitious but achievable goals for the day. I reward myself after achieving my goals. I am proud of myself and satisfied with what I did, and I can fully enjoy the rewards. Now, you do not have to wait until the end of the day. I juggle different topics and usually work on different blocks daily. Let's look at my day today. I set myself the goal to edit chapter 4 and 5. I rewarded myself at the end of this morning with a coffee after completing chapter 4. I am now working through this chapter (5). After chapter five, I will take a walk. Then I will get to my Viva defense preparation and read four academic papers as a preparation. Afterward, I am calling it a day and rewarding myself by meeting a very inspiring woman. It is important to stay disciplined and focused on completing the activity you want and rewarding yourself after. This concept is called Delayed Gratification or savoring and is picked up for example.

5.15 Making Difficult Things Less Difficult by Reverting

Another strategy is instead of doing the hard things and then practicing gratification later, make the hard things less hard. Often, if you look at a problem from a different distance or angle, you find new ways to solve a problem or get something done. However, complexity can make something difficult. Therefore, look for less complex ways to achieve your goal. I always remind myself of this famous quote that I twisted: "If the prophet does not come to the hill, the hill will need to go to the prophet."

Why am I saying it like that? We are so focused on seeing things a certain way that we believe they are set. They are realities we cannot change. These assumptions are like mountains, we believe we cannot touch them, but that is not true. By doing exactly that, questioning whether they are fixed, we can uncover new and easier ways.
I give you an example of how this advice helped me in my private life. I was in the hospital and was quite weak for weeks. I did not know how long it would take to recover. I did not go out that often because I was concerned about fainting. As a very sociable person, that was very hard for me and made me quite sad on some days. I thought about how I could change my situation. As I could not really get to my friends, I thought of how I could get them to me. I created a WhatsApp group and invited friends living in the region to a regular get-together/party in my apartment. In this way, they could meet great people and mingle, while

I meet the people dear to me and we all have a great time together.

This idea even led me to another idea regarding my business. I thought: Instead of going after my customers, how can I get them to come to me? I actually had a great idea of how to do it... But pssst...you will find that out soon! Here is an exercise to practice reverting:

EXERCISE: Identify three currently hard things for you and think of how you can revert them. Give them less difficult solutions.

5.16 Don't Chase, Attract

I am a romantic person, I admit. However, there is one thing I do not enjoy about some Hollywood and Bollywood movies. I really do not believe in unrequited love. I believe you cannot own people, catch people, or keep people. Either they love to be around you and want to stay or they don't. There is nothing you can do about it, and more importantly, you should not.

I like the thought of the authors Mali Apple and Joe Dunn in The Soulmate Experience. They suggest seeing other people like guests in your life. Now, why am I telling you that? I think a bit of chase and persuasion is okay and good. However, chasing should happen with certain boundaries. You should have a certain sense of self-worth. You are amazing, and you should know that. Why should you run after and love a person that does not think you are great and does not recognize your worth? That's why I think the glorification of unrequited love a la Romeo & Julia is unhealthy, and dangerous.

Tony Robbins articulates a similar opinion. I believe better than chasing is to be the best version of yourself that you can be. Typically, you attract people on the same frequency. This means, the better you take care of yourself, the better people you attract. There is this saying, "Throw your pearls before pigs." If someone does not recognize your worth, you might be a pearl and the other person the pig. I often see this phenomenon in dating females. Women sometimes start dating a partner slightly below their "level" because they believe this guy will be grateful. Interestingly, most times, the opposite happens; these guys do not know how lucky they are. The same thing happens in friendship or networking. Hence, the most successful strategy is to be happy with yourself and attract other people that are happy with themselves. These people will recognize your worth and will be grateful to have you and put in the effort. You do not need to convince them.

EXERCISE: Stop chasing so hard. You can do that at the beginning, but stop if they do not respond with mutual interest.

5.17 Why 'Trying' Sets You Up for Failure

As you already read earlier, words you think or tell others matter. There is one way many of us are cheating ourselves. Many of us use the word "try, „ which is very dangerous. When was the last time you thought or said, "I will try to finish this today!" And how did that usually end? At the end of the day, you did not complete what you wanted and told yourself, "Well, I did not finish, but I tried," and you ticked the item off in your brain. Saying you "tried" is the opposite of commitment. You are leaving the back door open because you do not want to commit, because of laziness, because you do not like the pressure, or because you are not sure if you can make it. With "trying," you are setting yourself up for failure.

EXERCISE: Observe your thoughts and words. Cut "trying" from your vocabulary and instead say "I will."

5.18 Journaling – Document Your Progress

Journaling massively helps you in all three aspects of the framework. Let me explain my journal structure below. I developed it over time. First, I think about what I am grateful for, which brings me to a positive state. If you FEEL grateful, you cannot be scared or depressed at the same time, remember!?

Then I write down what I achieved. If you are like me, then you are doing a lot all day and then at the end of the day, or the next day, you barely remember what you did. I write down all the things I achieved because I would not remember or recognize big parts of what I did, otherwise. It gives me a sense of achievement. Here I also document regular stuff that I do not like, such as doing the dishes. If you document it, it gives you more motivation to tackle such activities. You can even revisit what you did in the last week, and you will be surprised how much you achieved. It helps you to recognize your reverse gap better.

In the next section, I write down what I learned. This might be from something I did, advice from people or for me, I often document what I learned from books or courses.
Then in the next section, breakthroughs, I document things I did for the first time, major milestones, and most importantly, things that I find/found very hard. This section is one of the most important one for me. Then,

after, I have the section, To Learn: Here, I mostly document shortcomings or insights/stuff I learned that I need to implement now.

After that, I write down what makes me feel good and what does not make me feel good. I recommend you complete these sections as they will help you to get to know yourself better. More importantly, it will help you identify when you allowed someone to overstep your boundaries, and enable you to track your well-being and optimize your self-care.

My three wins of the day could be seen as a repetition of my breakthroughs. However, here it is more that I document what I am most proud of today. Then finally, I document three things I love about myself. These two last sections are important to improve your self-acceptance and to thank yourself for being you.

EXERCISE: Set up your journal template and journal in it; ideally every day. I am doing it on a remarkable, you can do it on your computer, iPad, or paper. Here is my journal structure. Feel free to adjust.
————————————
Templates:
JOURNAL
Priscilla's Template for a Day:

JOURNAL

Grateful for:
_____
_____

Achieved:
_____
_____

Learned:
_____
_____

Breakthrough:
_____
_____

To Learn:
_____
_____ _____

Makes me feel good:
_____
_____

Makes me feel bad:
_____
_____

My three wins of the day:

1. _____
2. _____
3. _____

Three things I love about myself:

1. _____
2. _____
3. _____

5.19 Meditation – Managing Your State

For me, personally, meditation is very important. I do not see that in a particular religious or spiritual way. There are many different practices out there.
I took on different meditation approaches that helped me to connect to myself. Feel free to adjust.
The main one I present here is adapted from Bishen Lakhiani.

EXERCISE: Try to follow my example: I sit crossed-legged somewhere where it is quiet and not too bright. If you are scared of falling asleep, use an alarm clock and set it for 20 minutes. You can make it shorter, but at the beginning, take some time. I switch off notifications and calls and select some meditation music that works for me on YouTube. I sit straight, shoulders back, my hands on my legs with palms to the sky.

1. COUNT: I breathe in deeply, breathe out and count 3, 3, 3 and see the numbers in front of me. I do the same again with 2, 2, 2, and then with 1, 1, 1.
2. RELAX: I breathe and while breathing out, I relax my eyelids. Then the next time, I breathe out, I relax the rest of my face, then my neck, and so forth.
3. DIVE: I imagine falling into the water (You can also choose to be in space, in a jungle, or wherever. it should feel like another world that is unlimited but where you feel comfortable.). I fall into the water. I feel calm there and swim. I am not far below the surface. I can feel the water and sun on my skin. I see the beautiful and colorful corals and fishes. With every stroke I make, I feel that dirt (negative thought) and injuries (pain) disappear from my skin and resolve in the water. My skin starts glowing slightly golden. I feel everything weighing heavily on me disappear; I am just me. I start counting from 1 to 10, and

while doing that, I am not far from the shore. I am leaving the surface, and I am diving through caves.

4. NOT YOU: I find a round cave with a rock in the middle. The cave wall in front of me is like a canvas. I see a lost, unhappy, and unsuccessful person in front of me. That is not the person I want to see. By moving my hand, I am breaking that picture like glass. It is not pleasant but it is important that you do not leave that part out, because seeing how you do not want to be drives you even more than just seeing how you want to be.

a. YOU: For beginners, you can pull up a new screenand visualize how you want to be and how you wantyour life to be. The more you can involve your senses and emotions, the more powerful.

b. YOU ADVANCED: This is when you are very good at meditating. Instead of visualizing pictures, you all ocate meanings to colors. I, for example, use green for health, red for love... Imagine, for example, a bright red screen. Expand the screen, so it is covering the whole cave so that the red has a bubble around it, like on a heater.Increase the intensity by turning an imaginary wheel. Feel that red sparkles come from the bubble and sur round you. Feel the energy coming   to you and going in side you. If you feel it is sufficient, collect all the energy inside you and imagine shooting it in one beam into the sky/space. It flowing down everywhere around the world. You can do that for different colors.

5. RETURNING: If you are done, jump into the water, swim out and dive up, while counting to five. Then tell yourself, "I am now better than I have been before."

Well, that is the basic meditation routine that works for me. For a long time, I thought about meditation as something for monks and spiritual people. Now I see it more as a tool for connecting to myself, improving empathy, happiness, and performance, and visualizing my life.

Chapter 6 – Moving Forward

As we said at the beginning of the book, we hope this book has helped you connect with yourself and provided you with the solid foundation you need to form beautiful and deep connections. Now, you are ready to take the next step forward, to read our second book, 'Supernetworker'. This second book will teach you how to connect yourself with others! I am happy to explore with you how to do that. Connecting with others is one of our greatest needs. Without connecting others we cannot survive, and with great relationships, you thrive. If you master how to build meaningful connections to other people successfully, you raise the bar again and will reach an entirely other level – in your personal life, your happiness, your (potential) relationship, friendship, and your professional life!!! Ideally, your business and personal life blend in with each other, because you enjoy both so much!

Now, what to expect? You will learn how to identify the amazing people you want to connect to, where to find them, how to connect with them, and how to build up and maintain amazing relationships. Does it sound like work for you? I promise you, it does not. After completing the second book, meeting new people will be one of your greatest joys in life – whether you are an extrovert or introvert. Watch out for the book release of the second book in the series: "Supernetworker"!

Much love, Richard and Priscilla

REFERENCE LIST

Feelings Wheel. feelingswheel.com.

Gray, John. Men are from Mars, Women are from Venus. HarperCollins Publisers, 2015.

Lakhiani, Vishen. Be Extraordinary. Mindvalley, https://home.mindvalley.com/quests/en/be-extraordinary

Lokkertsen, Alf [@thepresentpsychologist]. Photo of The Mood Meter. Instagram, January 16, 2022. https://www.instagram.com/p/CYzDhhUMPUt/.

Page, Oliver. "How to Leave Your Comfort Zone and Enter Your 'Growth Zone'." Positive Psychology, 24 November, 2020, https://positivepsychology.com/comfort-zone/.

Rao, Srikumar. The Quest For Personal Mastery. Mind-valley, https://www.mindvalley.com/personal-mastery.

Priscilla participating with the Cranfield School of Management sailing team at the One Ocean Regatta organized by the Bocconi Business School & Costa Smeralda Yacht Club Sardinia

Priscilla on Polo horse Furia

Richard Lee-Thai is a TEDx Speaker and passionate about empowering people with the skills and mindset to make meaningful connections throughout their lives.